mesopotamia
the truth

what was really happening
in the 'cradle of civilisation'

ian lawton

Rational Spirituality Press

First published in 2020 by Rational Spirituality Press.

All enquiries to be directed to www.rspress.org.

Copyright © Ian Lawton 2020. All rights reserved.

The rights of Ian Lawton to be identified as the Author of the Work have been asserted by him in accordance with the Copyright, Designs and Patents Act 1988.

No part of this book may be used or reproduced in any manner whatsoever (excluding brief quotations embodied in critical articles and reviews), nor by way of trade or otherwise be lent, resold, hired out, or otherwise circulated in any form of binding or cover other than that in which it's published, without the publisher's prior written consent.

A CIP catalogue record for this title is available from the British Library.

ISBN 978-0-9928163-8-4

Cover design by Ian Lawton.
Cover photograph by Rasoul Ali, licensed by dreamstime.com.
Author photograph by Simon Howson-Green.

Introducing the 'Prehistoric Truth' Series

This series of books – summaries of each of which can be found in the closing pages – deals with Giza, Atlantis and Mesopotamia respectively, and its title requires a little explanation. First, I chose the word *prehistoric* simply because *historic* alone would convey a false context. Yet all three do at least partly cover the period of humanity's development *after* written records came into being.

Second, and perhaps rather more contentious, is the choice of the word *truth* in the title both of the series and of the books themselves. This originally sprang from the fact that the first volume was named *Giza: The Truth* by Virgin Books some twenty years ago. But the continued creation and dissemination of wild, alternative theories about ancient human history and prehistory in the interim has led me to the conclusion that, just as in modern politics and life in general, there's so much 'fake news' around that a dose of reality is more than ever required.

Of course that doesn't, however, mean I believe myself to have a monopoly on truth in these matters. All I strive to do is research and write with the maximum integrity and scholarship of which I'm capable, and to present both sides of the coin where necessary and possible, so readers can make up their own minds about the validity or otherwise of my conclusions. Basically I'm just trying to reintroduce a little dose of sanity and discrimination into the various debates, so that people with little time to properly research these matters for themselves aren't led completely astray by outlandish ideas that have little basis in reality.

There is, after all, more than enough that we still don't properly understand about human prehistory, and new discoveries are being made all the time by professional historians and archaeologists. So we hardly need to invent apparent 'mysteries' that have little foundation… however much the human mind may be fascinated by such things.

CONTENTS

PREFACE   1

PART ONE: ANCIENT MESOPOTAMIA

1 INTRODUCTION   5

    Emergence; civilising elements (waterways and irrigation, shipping and transport, architecture and city-states, agriculture and farming, writing and printing, culture and the arts, legal and political systems, metalwork and smelting, schools and education, astronomy and mathematics, medicine, science in general, brewing); character; excavation, discovery and decipherment; reconstructing history (votive inscriptions, royal lists, law codes, court decisions); historical summary.

2 THE PANTHEON OF GODS   24

3 THE LITERARY TEXTS   30

4 THE SUMERIAN TEXTS   35

    Sumerian myths (the Eridu Genesis or the Flood Myth, Enki and Ninmah/Ninhursag or the Birth of Man, Enki and Ninki/Ninhursag or a Sumerian Paradise Myth, Inanna and Enki or the Transfer of the Arts of Civilisation from Eridu to Uruk, Enki and the World Order: the Organisation of Earth and its Cultural Processes, Inanna's Descent to the Netherworld, Dumuzi Texts, Enlil and Ninlil or the Birth of the Moon God, the Ninurta Myth or Lugal-E: the Deeds and Exploits of Ninurta, other myths); Sumerian epics (Enmerkar and the Lord of Aratta, Enmerkar and Ensukushsiranna, Lugalbanda epics, Gilgamesh epics, Gilgamesh and the Land of the Living, Gilgamesh, Enkidu and the Netherworld, Gilgamesh and Aka of Kish); Sumerian divine hymns (Hymn to Enlil, Hymn to Inanna as Warrior, Star and Bride, Hymn to Nanshe, other divine hymns); miscellaneous Sumerian texts (the Babel Story, the Gudea Temple Inscriptions, the Cursing of Akkad: the Ekur Avenged, Royal Love Songs).

5 THE AKKADIAN TEXTS   51

    Akkadian myths (the Epic of Creation or Enuma Elish or When on High, Erra/Nergal and Ishum, Nergal and Ereshkiga); Akkadian epics (Atrahasis or When Gods Instead of Men, the Epic of Gilgamesh, Adapa, Etana, the Epic of Anzu/Zu).

PART TWO: ZECHARIA SITCHIN

6 INTRODUCTION	65
7 SITCHIN'S SUPPOSED SCHOLARSHIP	69
8 WHAT'S IN A SHEM?	76

    Text extracts (Gilgamesh and the Land of the Living, Hymn to Inanna, Gudea Temple Inscriptions, Adapa, Etana, the Epic of Anzu, the Epic of Creation, Genesis 6:4 , Genesis 11:2-8 , Isiah 56:5, untraceable passages); conclusion.

9 SITCHIN'S COSMOLOGY AND 'PLANET X'	85

    The creation of Earth; visitors from elsewhere; more on 'planet Nibiru'; the search for 'Planet X'; life on Planet X; the 'Nibiru cataclysm'; conclusion.

10 SITCHIN'S PANTHEON OF GODS	105
11 CONCLUSION	108
SOURCE REFERENCES	110
BIBLIOGRAPHY	119
INDEX	120
PLATES SECTION	

LIST OF FIGURES

Figure 1: Ancient Mesopotamian Chronology   23
Figure 2: The Sumerian Pantheon   26
Figure 3: Cylinder Seal Drawing from 'The Twelfth Planet'   75

LIST OF PLATES

These are located at the end of the book.

1. The Great Ziggurat of Ur.
2. Assyrian frieze from King Assurnasirpal's palace at Nimrud.
3. Clay tablet with Akkadian cuneiform script.
4. Clay tablet with Sumerian pictographic script.
5. Planisphere K8538.

PREFACE

Most people have heard of the pyramids in Egypt. Many will have some awareness that there were 'cradles of civilisation' in China and India too. Probably less universally known is Ancient Mesopotamia, which can reasonably lay claim to be at least on a par with these others and, in some people's eyes, is pre-eminent.

The chapters that now make up this work were originally drafted in 1998 and published on my website as a series of papers in 2000. But, in conjunction with releasing revised versions of my first two books *Giza: The Truth* and *Atlantis: The Truth* (originally *Genesis Unveiled*), I've decided that these papers too deserve a proper airing in printed form – mainly with relatively minor edits – for a new generation, as the third volume in the 'Prehistoric Truth' series. After all there's no doubt that interest in ancient history and civilisations continues unabated, and with good reason. But much of what's presented in both mainstream and social media is somewhat alternative fare that, in an age where acceptance of fake news and conspiracy theories is all too common and somewhat lacking in the required level of discrimination, needs to be challenged – again, and again, and again. There is so much to be fascinated by in our human prehistory that doesn't require us to make up ill-founded nonsense.

Consequently Part 1 is a summary of the orthodox scholarly view of Ancient Mesopotamia, concentrating on the discovery of its various cities and on the wealth of literary and other texts that have been discovered in its ruins. Some of these show rather charmingly just how much basic human concerns, humour and so on have remained unaltered across five millennia. However the only reason I began to investigate the scholars' translations of these texts was because I wanted to check out for myself the work and claims of a

PREFACE

fellow author, Zecharia Sitchin, whose work had fascinated and inspired me when I was completely new to non-orthodox or 'alternative' history. Unfortunately on closer inspection I found his work rather less inspiring, so I feel I should say a few words about my motivation for going to some lengths to expose what I perceive as the weaknesses in his work in Part 2, instead of just ignoring it and moving on.

The reason is that, over the last quarter of a century, his books have had the same sort of impact worldwide as they originally had on me. They have persuaded a great many people that the Mesopotamian gods were flesh and blood visitors from another planet, who created the human race by genetic experimentation and who can and will return when the time is right – in essence, therefore, that we're a slave race under their total control. This dangerous proposition perpetuates the view that humanity must look outside of itself for its eventual salvation or destruction – whereas I strongly believe that, just as for each of us individually, our collective fate lies entirely in our own hands via faith in our own divinity.

One other factor is my fundamental disagreement with Sitchin over the age of the Giza Pyramids. In order to support his revised chronology of humankind, and his contention that these monuments were built as 'ground markers' for incoming space flights, it was he who first suggested that Colonel Richard Howard Vyse faked the 'quarry marks' in the Relieving Chambers in the Great Pyramid, some of which include the name of its builder, Khufu. On proper investigation this proves to be one of the most distorted and disingenuous pieces of supposed research I've ever had the misfortune to come across, and a full and highly detailed rebuttal of this nonsense can be found in *Giza: The Truth*.[1] Bearing in mind that it was this original attack by Sitchin that prompted so many other alternative Egyptologists to repeat his accusations without question – although fortunately now most of them have seen the light – this saga perhaps more than any other tells us a very great deal about the man and his work.

MESOPOTAMIA: THE TRUTH

Sitchin passed on in 2010, but let's be quite clear that this material does *not* represent a cowardly attack on a fellow researcher who is no longer around to defend themselves. Apart from some fairly substantial edits to chapter 9, the papers in Part 2 were freely available on my website for at least a decade to allow Sitchin to rebut them if he would. Yet, even though I've a pretty strong idea that he knew about them for some time, this is something he never attempted.

Ian Lawton
July 2020

SOME NOTES ON STYLE

Comments in square brackets in quotes are mine, for clarification, while ellipses are used to indicate the omission of intervening words, sentences or paragraphs that are repetitive or irrelevant.

PART ONE

ANCIENT MESOPOTAMIA

1

INTRODUCTION

EMERGENCE

Lying within the western regions of modern-day Iraq, Mesopotamia – literally 'the Land between the Rivers' – is the name given since ancient times to the great alluvial plain built up by the silt deposits of the Euphrates in the west and the Tigris in the east. It extends from north of Baghdad down to the mouth of the Persian Gulf, and is bordered in the north and east by the vast mountain ranges stretching down from Kurdistan to the Zagros, and in the west by the Syrian desert.

The land is rich and fertile, ensuring high yields for farmers across the ages. Indeed it has been identified with the biblical 'Garden of Eden', especially since the Euphrates is one of the rivers quoted in Genesis 2:14 as flowing out of it. However this is to over-simplify the matter. The annual flood levels are entirely dependent on the degree of inundation coming down from the surrounding mountain ranges, and this is highly variable – unlike, for example, the Nile plains in Northern Egypt. The resulting alternation between drought and devastating flood made the area at worst highly vulnerable to famine, and at best an unpredictable place to live. Small wonder, say the traditionalists, that the early settlers revered their gods and prayed so much for favourable conditions.

This unpredictability was coupled with the inhospitable terrain surrounding the plains, which harboured many well-protected potential enemies and ensured escape was difficult. Furthermore the land was lacking in fundamental resources for building work – stone, timber and metal were in short supply unless brought in from

INTRODUCTION

surrounding areas some distance away. It wasn't therefore the paradise for the earliest civilisations on Earth to develop and flourish that some commentators would have us believe.

Even orthodox opinion now understands that urbanisation actually began with a variety of stone settlements in Turkey, Syria and Palestine dating as far back as the 12th millennium BCE.[1] Nevertheless it was to be many millennia before the most identifiable elements of modern civilised life were introduced in Sumer – whose name is derived from the Babylonian name for Southern Mesopotamia – somewhere between the middle and end of the 5th millennium BCE. Certainly most scholars agree that the other most commonly discussed early civilisations emerged in Ancient Egypt to the southwest and in the Indus Valley to the east some time later, towards the end of the 4th millennium BCE.[2]

The dating process for Sumer works broadly along the following lines. Reliable links between the archaeological and documentary evidence can be established as far back as c. 2500 BCE. This date is then recessed somewhere between 1500 and 2000 years based on the extent of stratified remains unearthed before virgin soil is encountered in excavations of the oldest occupied sites. However the respected Assyriologist Samuel Noah Kramer, of the University of Chicago, has indicated that this approach is further confused by geological arguments about the extent to which the Persian Gulf at one time extended into Southern Mesopotamia, about the timing of its recession, and about the underlying levels of the water table on the land.[3] These factors can evidently render any assumption about reaching virgin soil inaccurate, and may imply a 'false bottom' that masks earlier evidence of civilisation.

CIVILISING ELEMENTS

In a number of books published in the 1950s and 60s, the most influential of which is *The Sumerians: their History, Culture and Character*, Kramer has provided what remains the most extensive catalogue of the elements of civilisation introduced by the Sumerians. Let us take a brief look at their achievements.[4]

MESOPOTAMIA: THE TRUTH

WATERWAYS AND IRRIGATION

In order for some stability to be brought to bear on the irrigation of this area, extensive and complex systems of canals, weirs, dikes and reservoirs were built; these feats required advanced engineering skills, including accurate surveying and measurement. Furthermore these waterways required considerable annual maintenance to ensure they didn't become clogged up with silt. Such tasks required significant levels of co-operation between neighbours over an extended area. Indeed the orthodox view is that it was this very necessity that led to the emergence of civilisation in the area.

SHIPPING AND TRANSPORT

Given their reliance on waterways, it comes as no surprise to find that the Sumerians list many types of shipping vessel in their records. Kramer also supports the relatively modern view that from early times they were undertaking significant sea voyages – assumed until recently to be impossible at that time – not least so as to engage in trade with places such as Egypt and Ethiopia in order to acquire materials that their own region didn't provide.[5] According to the current orthodoxy they were also the first to introduce the wheel, from which they developed both the cart and chariot.

ARCHITECTURE AND CITY-STATES

These developed from the smaller towns and villages at the latest by the start of the 3rd millennium BCE, and housed populations of anything up to 100–200,000 people. The complexity of housing construction varied according to status, with the poor occupying single-story houses built usually of reinforced clay or mud bricks, while the better-off enjoyed grander dwellings of two or occasionally even three stories. However the concept of town planning was not particularly advanced, with private houses muddled together along usually narrow and jumbled streets and alleyways. Nevertheless the imposing and often monumental stepped temple or *ziggurat* of the patron god, and in later times the palace of the ruler – the *ensi* or *lugal* – were splendid affairs made of more expensive materials, and highly decorated inside and out

INTRODUCTION

with columns, arches and mosaics. The most impressive part-surviving structure is the Great Ziggurat of Ur (see Plate 1).

These buildings, sometimes combined with large and ornate city gates, wide boulevards and walkways, and central public squares that were a focal point for recreation, dominated the city. So successful was this prototype of civilised life that in subsequent millennia the city-state thrived from the Indus Valley in the east through to the Mediterranean in the west, based largely on the Sumerian model. Indeed our modern, city-based culture owes much to this original Sumerian influence – as against that of, for example, Ancient Egypt, which never adopted the city-state concept.

AGRICULTURE AND FARMING

There is evidence that the Sumerians experimented with both crops and livestock, introducing new varieties and strains of both that were not originally native to the area. Detailed instructions about agricultural activities throughout the year have been found on a tablet called the *Farmer's Almanac*.[6]

WRITING AND PRINTING

As far as we're currently aware the Sumerians were the first to develop a proper and widespread system of writing. They achieved this by imprinting clay tablets using a stylus. A form of printing was a similar first, whereby they carved 'negative' images onto 'cylinder seals' – stone cylinders usually between 2 and 6 centimetres long – which could then be repeatedly rolled over fresh clay to produce the 'positive' inscription. As forerunners of the rings used to imprint wax seals in later times they were used to identify possessions such as pottery, to seal written tablets to guarantee their authenticity, and to protect other valuables via clay stoppers on containers such as bottles, urns and leather bags.

With details of over 6000 already published, and many more residing in unpublished private collections, they provide an abundant source of information, with scenes portraying both mortals and gods – usually identified by horned headgear – and, later on, including inscriptions.[7]

CULTURE AND THE ARTS

Not only did the Sumerians produce complex stone sculptures, elaborate stylised friezes (see Plate 2), inscribed stelae, highly decorated pottery and beautiful clothing, but they also developed musical instruments such as the harp and lyre that were used to accompany the recital of their many epic literary works. They developed the concept of the library, assiduously collecting and cataloguing their mass of not only literary but also administrative, scientific and historiographic texts. There are also some indications that they indulged in vigorous debates both in public and private.

LEGAL AND POLITICAL SYSTEMS

Textual evidence indicates that they had a form of congress or assembly for making key political decisions using a consensual approach. Moreover that they held courts to make legal judgements over such things as house ownership, divorce and inheritance settlements, and slave rights. This legal and political system was at least in later times enshrined in a regularly published *Law Code* – effectively the earliest 'bills of rights' – which formed the prototype for later Greek and Roman systems. That they also developed some understanding of economics is attested by evidence of price-setting agreements.

METALWORK AND SMELTING

The Sumerians used many metals in the construction of buildings, household objects and jewellery, such as gold, silver, tin, lead, copper and bronze. They were also familiar with a wide variety of techniques for working with metals, such as annealing, granulation, riveting and filigree.

SCHOOLS AND EDUCATION

Centres of scholarship or *edubbas* were set up in most city-states at the latest by the middle of the 3rd millennium BCE. Primarily these provided education for the offspring of the better-off, and their main aim was to train the pupils to become specialist scribes. Given the complexities of the Sumerian language that by then existed,

INTRODUCTION

graduating from the *edubba* was no mean feat. Learning how to write the language, made harder because it wasn't alphabetic or phonetic, was a multi-stage process: students started with vocabulary, for example learning and copying 'scientific' lists of botanical, zoological and mathematical words, each of which could extend into the hundreds or even thousands; they then progressed to mastering the complexities of Sumerian written grammar.

But the *edubba* was at the same time a 'centre of learning' where, as now, lecturers and senior scholars also engaged in original research to add to the extant body of knowledge in many areas. Furthermore, even in the literary areas, writing wasn't only directed towards learning, copying and preserving, but also towards the occasional creation of new epics.

ASTRONOMY AND MATHEMATICS

The Sumerians developed a highly-advanced quasi-sexagesimal system of mathematics, and a highly accurate lunar calendar with adjustments to reconcile it to the solar calendar. As to their broader astronomical knowledge, orthodox opinion holds that they knew of only about 25 stars that were presented in simple lists, and that their knowledge of the other planets in our solar system was limited or non-existent. However as we'll see in Part 2 this view has been challenged by at least one prominent alternative author.

MEDICINE

The majority of the hundreds of medical tablets currently excavated date only to the early part of the 1st millennium BCE, and are written in later Akkadian script – of which more later. Nevertheless these utilise many Sumerian words and phrases that indicate their heritage, and a few similar tablets have been found that date as far back as the start of the 2nd millennium BCE. It has been suggested that these ancient pharmacopoeias, which describe a variety of illnesses and cures, would probably be remarkably similar to those compiled only a couple of hundred years ago. But although the texts describe fundamentally practical procedures, these tend to be couched in a moral framework that views disease as a punishment for wrongdoing. As a result we regularly come across 'supernatural' elements in Sumerian medical thinking, including for example exorcism.

It would also appear that their medical knowledge didn't develop a great deal over several millennia. However this shouldn't detract from the evidence that they researched a great many herbal remedies, many of which apparently worked, and indeed they were perhaps more aware than many modern practitioners of the 'healthy mind, healthy body' approach, and the possibility of psychosomatic illness.

SCIENCE IN GENERAL

Both the Sumerians and their successors in Mesopotamia were highly curious and lovers of knowledge, often just for its own sake. They were particularly methodical, and therefore arguably made good scientists. To suggest as some have that Mesopotamian science consisted only of a series of 'lists' is almost certainly to do it a grave disservice. Moreover, although no textbooks have yet been found, evidence suggests a strong reliance on lectures for teaching and explanation.

BREWING

Brewing was an issue of such importance to the Sumerians that it had its own patron goddess, Ninkasi, or 'the Lady who Fills the Mouth'. Indeed one medical remedy asserts: 'If a man has a stone of the bladder this man will drink beer, and the stone will dissolve; if this man instead of drinking beer drinks much water, he will go to his destiny.' Even if they were wrong, at least he'd die happy…

CHARACTER

So what of the *character* of the Sumerians? This can be neglected when we're engrossed in archaeological and linguistic details, but Kramer's view is that they loved life and wanted to extend it as much as possible – at least in part because they believed death led them to a rather uninviting and dreary netherworld.[8] He suggests that in adopting this approach they appear to have had little concept of a utopian heaven, or an abominable hell for that matter, nor indeed of reincarnation. They certainly didn't develop anything like the esoteric worldviews of the Ancient Egyptian and Vedic civilisations.

Overall then one does form the impression that they were fundamentally materialistic, competing aggressively for pre-eminence, social standing and prestige. Combined with the fact that they identified with their city-state more than with Sumer itself, this led to perpetual wars between city-states in the struggle for ascendancy – to such an extent that dominant rulers always struggled to keep Sumer united. Indeed their civilisation was ultimately brought down by being weakened from within, rendering them vulnerable to attack from external invaders. Vanity and lack of humility were also highly evident in their make-up, especially in the self-laudatory royal hymns of the *ensis*. Yet they seemed at the same time to have had a great sense of morality, prizing truth and compassion, law and order, justice and freedom, wisdom and learning, and courage and loyalty. They were, indeed, an enigmatic people.

EXCAVATION, DISCOVERY AND DECIPHERMENT

The Mesopotamian city-states were repeatedly abandoned and reoccupied in ancient times. Either water levels rose, or over time the rivers changed their course – for example, in places the course of the Euphrates is now as much as 50 kilometres to the west of its position *c.* 2000 BCE[9] – either of which could render their continued occupation untenable. Moreover the in-house rivalry for supremacy, coupled with invasions by foreign usurpers, meant that they were often attacked and destroyed. When sites were later reoccupied, the old ruins were simply levelled and used as foundations. Hence the 'levels' referred to by archaeologists.

When they were finally abandoned the mainly mud-brick buildings collapsed, leaving piles of rubble that rapidly became covered with sand or vegetation. Despite their often impressive size, the resulting mounds or *tells* rising out of what was now primarily arid desert attracted little attention over the intervening millennia – until a few travellers in the 17th century began retrieving the odd brick, and isolated fragments of tablets bearing 'unknown inscriptions'. Western interest in the area grew, and in 1842 the French consul in Mosul, Paul Emil Botta, undertook the first proper excavation at Kuyunjik in Northern Mesopotamia. When initially nothing was found he switched his attentions to nearby Khorsabad, and was duly rewarded when he discovered the ruined palace of the Assyrian King Sargon II, dating to the latter part of the 8th century BCE.

Then in 1845 the British archaeologist Sir Austen Henry Layard began digging at both Nimrud and Kuyunjik, and struck gold. The latter site turned out to be the infamous biblical city of Nineveh, and there he uncovered the ruins of the Royal Library of King Ashurbanipal, the great-grandson of Sargon II. This contained literally thousands of tablet-fragments that would subsequently prove to be collations of the vast body of literary and administrative texts of the Ancient World, written in the wedge-shaped or *cuneiform* script of the period (see Plate 3). In fact Layard and his colleagues, Hormuzd Rassam and George Smith, continued their work at this site for the next 25 years, unearthing a huge number of clay plaques. However we should be careful here, because many sloppily written books fail to make the distinction between the numbers of *fragments* found as against the number of complete *tablets* that might represent – leaving one with the initial impression that far more of the latter are in our possession than is in fact the case. Nevertheless the 25-30,000 fragments found in the ruins of Ashurbanipal's library were still estimated to represent as many as 10,000 complete tablets. Similarly valuable sources were the libraries at Ashur, unearthed by a German team from 1902-14.

However we're jumping ahead of ourselves. At the time of Layard's initial discovery the unusual script on the tablets was undeciphered. In fact to trace how it was decoded we need to go back to the trilingual inscriptions found on the ruins of a magnificent palace at Persepolis in Iran. From the writings of various travellers

INTRODUCTION

it's clear that these were known to the Western world as far back as the beginning of the 16th century, but it took until the end of the 18th century for scholars to establish that the first language or 'Class' was Old Persian, and semi-alphabetic. Meanwhile translation of the other two proved impossible, because the inscriptions were too short and consisted of mainly of proper names.

Fast forward to the 1830s, when a British Army officer who was to become arguably the most influential figure in the understanding of cuneiform script – culminating in his heading up the Department of Oriental Antiquities at the British Museum – entered the fray. Sir Henry Creswicke Rawlinson started work on some similar trilingual inscriptions carved into the rock outcrops at Behistun, which were far lengthier and therefore allowed greater scope for understanding the languages involved. Often risking his own neck because the inscriptions were several hundred feet off the ground, he meticulously copied them down over a number of years. By 1850, in conjunction with the Irish Assyriologist Edward Hincks and his French-German counterpart Jules Oppert, the decipherment of both the first and second Classes of script – the latter proving to be Elamite – was more or less complete. This led to the three becoming known as 'cuneiform's holy triad'.

They then of course turned their attention to the third Class, and realised that the huge number of symbols and variants thereof were caused by the fact that the language and its symbols were both syllabic *and* ideographic, the latter meaning that whole words could be written with one symbol. They also realised it was polyphonic, in that the same sign could have more than one sound or value. The jigsaw was completed by the discovery of syllabaries at Nineveh, which ancient scribes had prepared to assist understanding of the language. So by 1859 Oppert was able to publish a study of the language now known as Akkadian, which was so authoritative that the foundations of its understanding were complete. This launched a tidal wave of scholarly effort directed towards the increasing numbers of Akkadian tablets being found at Nineveh and elsewhere, the translation of which is now reasonably assured from a linguistic point of view.

However at about this time Hincks was already turning his attention to another mystery. The Assyro-Babylonians who inhabited Mesopotamia for the bulk of the 1st and 2nd millennia BCE were a Semitic race – this term deriving from the name of Noah's son Shem, from whom all Semites are thought to be descended. Yet the syllabic values of the Akkadian script couldn't be linked with Semitic counterparts, and he began to suspect that it must have derived from one developed by previous, non-Semitic inhabitants of Mesopotamia. Then in 1869 Oppert delivered a lecture in which he noted that inscriptions contained the phrase 'King of Sumer and Akkad' – and thus the Sumerians were formally rediscovered.

Any lingering doubts about the existence of this non-Semitic race were soon dispelled by the recommencement of excavations, this time in Southern Mesopotamia. In 1877 a French team began work at Telloh, which is now recognised as the Sumerian city of Lagash, which were continued by successive French teams right through to 1933. In 1887 an American team began work at Nippur, where over the next decade one of the largest sources of mainly Sumerian texts was unearthed – for example, some 30,000 tablet-fragments were removed from its sacerdotal library. In the first half of the twentieth century a German team excavating at Uruk, the biblical Erech, discovered around a thousand tablet-fragments dating as far back as the start of the 3rd millennium BCE. As yet these remain the oldest found, and they contain the earliest forms of Sumerian 'pictographic' script (see Plate 4). They also dug a proper test pit some 20 metres deep, which assisted the understanding of chronological development at the site from the earliest times. Meanwhile another German team worked at Shuruppak from 1902-3; a French team at Kish from 1912-14; an Anglo-American team again at Kish from 1923-33, under Stephen Langdon; and a British team at Ur – the biblical home of the patriarch Abraham – from 1922-34, under Sir Leonard Woolley.

Having taken some time to build up from humble beginnings, by the time of WWII the Iraqi Directorate of Antiquities had become a

INTRODUCTION

well-established outfit quite capable of organising its own excavations. One of its earliest and most notable achievements was the rediscovery of Eridu, the oldest known Sumerian city, in 1946. Here they excavated the patron god Enki's temple down to its earliest incarnation *c.* 4000 BCE, although unfortunately no tablets came to light. Admittedly in the 1950s an American team under Harvard professor Thorkild Jacobsen was allowed back to Nippur, where they uncovered two temples dedicated to the patron deities Enlil and Inanna, and around a thousand more mainly literary tablet-fragments. But since then the responsibility for continued excavation in Mesopotamia has rested primarily, although not exclusively, with the Iraqis themselves.

To return to the issue of the Sumerian language, once tablets had been found that contained non-Akkadian cuneiform script – for example, at Nippur and Uruk – the decipherers faced a new challenge, although in some senses it was an easier task than before. The Akkadians and later Assyrians didn't just borrow from Sumerian script, they also treasured its literary inheritance. So in their *edubbas* they copied hundreds of Sumerian texts into their own script to preserve them, albeit with some political and religious editing over the centuries that we'll consider in chapter 5. They also prepared detailed Sumerian-Akkadian dictionaries and lexicons that considerably assisted Sumerologists in the translation of words and understanding of grammar. Many of these had already been found at Nineveh, but excavations at Nippur yielded numerous lexicons concerned with Sumerian vocabulary and grammar in its own right. This meant that by the beginning of the twentieth century scholars such as Francois Thureau-Dangin, Arno Poebel, Archibald Sayce, Rudolph Brunow and John Prince were able to compile rudimentary, modern, Sumerian lexicons. However the language is complex, and much more progress has been achieved in the interim.

As a result of the profusion of archaeological activity over the last two centuries, several hundred thousand tablet-fragments have now been unearthed – some even put the estimate as high as half a million. The fact that so many fragile tablets have survived at all, albeit fragmented, is in part due to the unfortunate fate that befell many of the sites in which they were preserved. When the city-states were attacked by enemies they were usually set on fire, which meant that although buildings were destroyed, the clay tablets were fired and better preserved for archaeologists to find.

This wealth of written information is backed up by hundreds of pictorial representations of early events engraved on temple walls, stone stelae and decorative friezes. Although some are no doubt housed in private collections, the majority of them can be viewed in publicly-accessible collections all around the world – for example in the British Museum, the Louvre, the Archaeological Museum in Istanbul, the Iraq Museum in Baghdad, the Vorderasiatische Museum in Berlin, the Friedrich-Schiller University in Jena and the Philadelphia University Museum.

Many of the texts that the tablets represent are still incomplete to varying degrees, and many more fragments undoubtedly remain undiscovered. But we already have a vast inheritance, and it's not only due to the efforts of the linguists who originally deciphered the various scripts that we're able to read them now. Arguably even greater scholarly effort has had to be expended in piecing together the fragments. This job is far more difficult than completing a conventional jigsaw. Remember that the pieces were often found at different times by different expeditions, and sometimes taken to be housed in different collections in different countries. Imagine that you have a jigsaw where you don't know the complete size and shape, where the pieces can be mutilated at the edges, and where the picture is very uniform – that is, all writing.

The only saving grace was that multiple copies of especially literary texts were often found – many of which were, for example, exercise tablets from *edubbas* that were preserved for us by being dumped and used as in-fill for the foundations of later buildings. Although this in turn presented problems in that the scholars had to attempt to identify any errors made by poor or inexperienced students, it did mean that, where one copy was incomplete, another might fill in the gaps if it overlapped enough to be recognisable as the same text. One other factor that assisted the identification process was that colophons were often inscribed at the end of each tablet to identify them. These recorded the title of the text, which was always based on the opening line; the number of the tablet within the series, which was the equivalent to a page or chapter number; and an 'identifying phrase' that was usually made up of several lines of text from the end of one tablet that would be repeated at the beginning of the next.

All in all, decades of painstaking work has been undertaken on Akkadian and Sumerian tablets by scholars such as the already mentioned Jacobsen, Kramer, Langdon and Smith, along with Stephanie Dalley, Adam Falkenstein, Alexander Heidel, Leonard King, Wilfred Lambert, Alan Millard and Ephraim Speiser, among others. This has ensured that the multiple pieces of the various jigsaws have been progressively slotted into place. Among the wealth of information revealed has been concrete proof that some of the biblical versions of early events in humankind's history are edited highlights of far earlier versions that contain considerably greater detail. Most obvious of these is the story of the Flood and its hero Noah, but we'll examine all of the main Sumerian and Akkadian texts in subsequent chapters.

RECONSTRUCTING HISTORY

There are two main paths available to those who want to reconstruct Ancient Mesopotamian history. The first is the conventional archaeological one of digging down into successive layers of remains at key sites. Anyone who has watched the popular television programme 'Time Team' in the UK will by now have become familiar with this approach, which involves digging test trenches, then the various artifacts discovered at each level are dated by cross-referencing them to finds at other sites. However when archaeologists began their excavations in Ancient Mesopotamia they didn't have any yardsticks because the whole area was a green-field site. So what could they use for assistance with dating?

Radiocarbon dating of animate remains is often used under these circumstances, but it tends to be more useful for older sites where accuracy to, say, the nearest couple of hundred years is acceptable. In Ancient Mesopotamia scholars were looking for greater precision, but they had a second path to follow that's not always available elsewhere, especially when going back as far as the 3rd and 4th millennia BCE: and that was, of course, the written evidence. Apart from the literary texts we'll concentrate on in subsequent chapters, the excavated tablets were also found to contain administrative and historiographic texts that have provided scholars with an invaluable source of information with which to construct a chronological framework. The following are the major types of non-literary document that have been bequeathed to us, as listed by Kramer:[10]

VOTIVE INSCRIPTIONS

From at least as far back as *c.* 2750 BCE the *ensis* of the various city-states had personal memorials inscribed just about everywhere – on stone and clay tablets, on building bricks and blocks, on stelae and plaques, on statues and statuettes, and on bowls and vases. Echoing the self-laudatory tone of their hymns, these inscriptions listed the *ensi's* major accomplishments in terms of subjugating other races and cities, and of building, rebuilding and refurbishing temples and palaces. Not only do these often include useful descriptions of religious offerings and ceremonies, but they also indicate which gods were being worshipped in a given place at a given time. The prime examples are:

- The *Sargon Inscriptions*, which form a contemporary record of all the inscriptions on statues and stelae in the reign of the first king of the Akkad Dynasty *c.* 2300 BCE. They were meticulously prepared by a scribe and found on tablets at Nippur.
- The *Gudea Temple Inscriptions*, which consist of two long tablets of 54 columns each, found at the city of Lagash over which Gudea ruled *c.* 2100 BCE.

Most important these sometimes include 'date-formulas', which

INTRODUCTION

were used from c. 2500 BCE onwards by Sumerian scribes. These commemorate the date of significant religious and political events, although not via an *absolute* year reference, but by the number of years *into* an *ensi's* reign in which they occurred.

ROYAL LISTS

By contrast these contain lists dealing with more than one ruler. Examples include:

- The *Tummal Inscription*, which catalogues the rulers in charge of the building and rebuilding of the patron god Enlil's temple complex at Nippur.
- The *Lagash Inscriptions*, which list the various rulers of that city, starting with Ur-Nanshe c. 2500 BCE.
- The *Sumerian King List*, undoubtedly the most important list of all, which records the rulers of all the Sumero-Akkadian dynasties *except* those of Lagash and Larsa – perhaps because these weren't regarded as ruling the whole of Sumer-Akkad. Compiled from about 15 different and fragmented copies found mainly at Larsa and Nippur, this list has played a pivotal role in the development of the chronology of Ancient Mesopotamia – albeit that the task was complicated by the dynasties sometimes overlapping considerably.

LAW CODES

We have already mentioned these briefly; the major examples are:

- The *Urukagina Reform Text*, prepared at the instigation of the *ensi* of Lagash c. 2350 BCE, describes how the common people were freed from the burden of unnecessary taxes, and records laws for the punishment of various crimes.
- The *Law Code of Ur-Nammu*, the founder of the 3rd Dynasty of Ur c. 2100 BCE.
- The *Law Code of Lipit-Ishtar*, a ruler of the Isin Dynasty c. 1900 BCE.
- The *Law Code of Hammurabi*, the great conqueror who

established the Assyro-Babylonian Empire in the early 18th century BCE.

The last three all follow a similar format, with a prologue, the laws themselves – which lay out basic rules regarding such issues as property, slaves, marriage and inheritance – and an epilogue.

ROYAL LETTERS

The earliest of these date to *c.* 2400 BCE. Particularly useful is the correspondence of the last ruler of the 3rd Dynasty of Ur, Ibbi-Sin, revealing how his one-time courtier turned rival Ishbi-Erra built up the Dynasty of Isin until Ibbi-Sin was forced to capitulate at the beginning of the 2nd millennium BCE.

COURT DECISIONS

Also known as *ditillas*, these contain judgements regarding divorce, land, livestock and other disputes.

Admittedly some of these records were of an administrative nature, and assisted the understanding of cultural more than of chronological history. What is more even the historiographic records were insufficient on their own. However, when enough of them had come together, it proved possible to cross-reference them to other, more recent, known historical events and then to try to work backwards and plot an absolute timeline.

From 911 BCE onwards the resultant chronology is more or less exact in that it was possible to corroborate astronomical records of eclipses on Assyrian tablets with those recorded by the Greek Ptolemy. Going further back it isn't perfect, not least because some of the pieces of written evidence seem to contradict each other, while it's not always clear whether events are consecutive or overlapping. Nevertheless the current orthodox view is that, while dates going back to *c.* 3000 BCE can vary from source to source, the variation isn't material for the purposes of most research.

HISTORICAL SUMMARY

The Sumerians were pre-eminent, especially in Southern

INTRODUCTION

Mesopotamia, in the 4th and most of the 3rd millennia BCE. However for much of that time they co-existed with the Akkadians, so-called after their capital city of Agade or Akkad, who lived to the north. They in turn came to dominate the whole area in the latter part of the 3rd millennium BCE. But their reign was short-lived, lasting only a few hundred years before they in turn were usurped by the Assyrians, also known as the Babylonians after their capital city. Hence the use of compound terms such as 'Sumero-Akkadian' and 'Assyro-Babylonian'. Note also that scholars of Ancient Mesopotamian history are often referred to as 'Assyriologists' because Assyrian artifacts and texts were those first discovered during excavations, even though the term is now used to cover the study of earlier civilisations too.

In order that the various references to periods and rulers in subsequent chapters may be placed in context, the more detailed results of the chronological reconstruction referred to above are summarised in Figure 1. The dates are taken from the chronology prepared by Georges Roux, a former medical officer with the Iraq Petroleum Company who became so fascinated by the history of the region that he turned Assyriologist. Although his excellent reference work *Ancient Iraq* was originally published in 1964, this data is taken from the updated third edition of 1992.[11]

Period or Era	BCE	Description and Key Events
Prehistoric	Pre 3000	Earliest occupation at Eridu *c.* 5000 BCE.
Early Dynastic (Sumerian)	3000-2300	Sumerian dominance, primarily under dynasties of Kish I-II-III-IV, Uruk I-II-III, Ur I-II. Heroes of epics rule in early dynasties: e.g. Etana and Aka during Kish I, and Enmerkar, Lugalbanda and Gilgamesh during Uruk I.
Dynasty of Akkad (plus Gutium and Ur III)	2300-2000	Akkadians from the north conquer Sumer under Sargon the Great *c.* 2334 BCE. Gutians from further north conquer Sumer-Akkad *c.* 2150 BCE.

Period or Era	BCE	Description and Key Events
		Ur III briefly comes to prominence c. 2112 BCE until fall of Ur c. 2004 BCE signals end of Sumer's predominance as political force in Mesopotamia.
Isin-Larsa	2000-1750	Dynasty of Isin commences under Ishbi-Erra.
Old Assyro-Babylonian	1750-1600	Hammurabi conquers whole of Assyria and Mesopotamia and rules from Babylon, signalling final collapse of weakened Sumer as independent political force. Assyro-Babylonian Empire forms a Semitic state built on a Sumerian foundation.
Kassite-Hittite	1600-1150	Babylon conquered by Hittites c. 1595 BCE.
Middle Assyro-Babylonian	1150-750	Babylon continues its pre-eminence.
Late (Neo-) Assyro-Babylonian	750-500	Sargon II and Sennacherib transfer power to Nineveh c. 700 BCE; set up Royal Library that contains copies of many Sumerian texts. Ashurbanipal adds to library at Nineveh c. 650 BCE. Sumerian cultural influence still in evidence; like Latin now, Sumerian language still used in some scholarly and liturgical documents even though it hadn't been spoken for over a millennia.

Figure 1: Ancient Mesopotamian Chronology

2

THE PANTHEON OF GODS

The gods played a crucial role in Sumer, both for the nation and for individuals, and most Sumerians appear to have had a personal god or gods with whom they forged a special relationship. Their texts and stelae indicate that, like so many other cultures, they looked to their deities for protection and assistance in all things, while also blaming them or looking upon it as a punishment – just or otherwise – when things went wrong. As with the endurance of their literature these gods, with some amendments, continued to be worshipped right through to the late Assyro-Babylonian period. Since they play a crucial role in the literary texts that we'll consider in subsequent chapters, it's appropriate that we take time out to consider the key figures.

The collective name most often given to the Sumerian pantheon is the *Anunnaki*, although another name, the *Igigi*, is also encountered. These two appear to be interchangeable in some texts, although in others there are inconsistent and conflicting roles accorded to each as greater or lesser gods. For example, in *Atrahasis* the Anunnaki are the 'great gods' while the Igigi 'do the work'. By contrast, in the *Epic of Creation*, in *Erra and Ishum* and in the *Epic of Anzu* the Igigi are made out to be superior, the first two referring to 'the Igigi of heaven and the Anunnaki of the Abzu' – the latter term referring to 'the deep', sometimes regarded as the 'watery underworld'.

The number of gods in the – or each – pantheon also differs from text to text, with them sometimes referring to 'fifty great gods' and sometimes to as many as three hundred. It is likely that this confusion arises because of changing roles allocated to various pantheons over time as part of a 'creative editing' process underpinned by political and religious motives – something we encounter in the sacred texts of all religions and cultures, and to which we'll return in the next chapter. For example, it appears that the Igigi tend to be the younger gods who appear primarily in the later Akkadian works, while the Anunnaki are the older great gods of the Sumerians.

This confusion about different pantheons and their potential hierarchical structure permeates most Assyriologists' work. In *The Chaldean Account of Genesis*, published in 1876, George Smith – who succeeded Henry Rawlinson as the head of the Department of Oriental Antiquities at the British Museum – describes a pantheon of 'twelve great gods' who, despite having been given somewhat different names in his day, are broadly the same figures, with similar associations, that we currently regard as having been pre-eminent.[1] He suggests the hierarchy then proceeded through a further fifty gods *before* the level of the Igigi, and then *finally* the Anunnaki.

By contrast Samuel Kramer describes the 'seven gods who decree the fates'.[2] He suggests these are probably made up of four 'creative gods' – An who rules heaven, Enlil the air or atmosphere, Enki water, and Ninhursag Earth; and of three 'astral deities' – Nanna associated with the Moon, Utu with the Sun, and Inanna usually with Venus. As with Smith they're followed by 'fifty great gods', but Kramer identifies these with the Anunnaki – as 'children of An' – while relegating the Igigi to a 'relatively minor role'.

What is clear is that there are a number of key players in this pluralistic pantheon of anthropomorphic gods who appear time and again in Ancient Mesopotamian literature and sculpture. In Figure 2 I've attempted to piece together a 'family tree' from the texts, not because this is a strictly correct or appropriate way of looking at them, but because this approach makes them come to life and puts them into some sort of context.[3] Of course assembling the apparent relationships between them is hugely complicated by a number of

THE PANTHEON OF GODS

factors: the gods' apparently protracted lifespans that lead to significant overlap; the multiple liaisons between them to produce children, including incestuous relationships involving brothers, sisters, children and grandchildren – which is in fact a common behaviour pattern adopted by the pantheons of most polytheistic cultures around the world; and the repeated editing of texts over millennia.

As a result the pantheon shown in Figure 2 shouldn't be regarded as anything more than a guide to introduce the major deities to those new to the subject. It should also be pointed out that the most likely interpretation of the texts is that as groups the Anunnaki and the later Igigi were regarded as subservient to the major deities listed below.

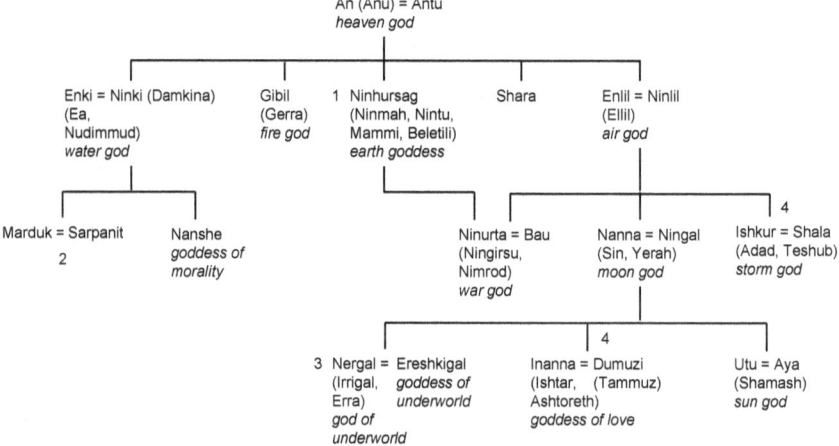

Figure 2: The Sumerian Pantheon

For consistency and ease of understanding I've tried to use the original Sumerian names of gods, people and places – and also the most up-to-date renderings thereof – not only here but also throughout subsequent chapters, including when commenting on the later Akkadian texts. The family tree does however indicate the most commonly found alternative names in brackets, especially the Akkadian versions used through to the end of the Assyro-Babylonian epoch. It also attempts to show the relationships between long-term consorts, and the main associations of gods with the elements and so forth. The following notes that accompany it contain various points of detail, especially indicating the areas of greatest uncertainty:

1. Ninhursag appears to be Enlil's consort in that they're Ninurta's parents, and Enki's consort in *A Sumerian Paradise Myth*. Yet overall she doesn't appear to be anyone's permanent consort. The continual editing of texts, the assimilation of one god with another at various times, and the polygamous and incestuous nature of most relationships, mean that we shouldn't get too hung up on such details.
2. Marduk is only recorded as Enki's son in the *Epic of Creation* and, given that he only came to prominence in the late Assyro-Babylonian period, the importance attached to him by some commentators must be viewed with some scepticism. Note also that he's so well known by this, his Akkadian name, that I've made an exception and used it throughout; his original Sumerian name was Asalluhe.
3. Nergal and Ninurta are sometimes assimilated with each other, probably because in *Enlil and Ninlil* Nergal is reported as their second son and Ninurta isn't mentioned, while in the later *Erra (Nergal) and Ishum* the former is again reported as Enlil's son. Occasionally Nergal is also assimilated with Gibil.
4. These two are sometimes recorded as direct offspring of An – Ishkur in the *Epic of Anzu*, Inanna in the *Epic of Gilgamesh*. However Ereshkigal is consistently recorded as Inanna's sister, similarly Utu as her brother, so if she were to shift up the generations arguably they should do likewise. Note also that gods are often misleadingly described as the 'son or daughter of An' as a poetic metaphor, perhaps to indicate that they're part of the main pantheon. The determination of his main offspring as shown is based on more substantial statements.

Despite the controversies over elements of detail, it's clear that certain gods in the Sumerian pantheon stood head and shoulders above the others, especially in earlier times – namely An, Enlil, Enki and Ninhursag. It is also clear that the relative importance of various gods changed over time. Kramer suggests that as the father of the gods An was originally the head of the pantheon – as portrayed, for example, in pictographic texts found at Uruk dating to *c.* 3000 BCE – but this position was subsequently transferred to Enlil. The latter has built a widespread reputation for bringing devastation to humankind – for example with the Flood – but Kramer suggests this is misplaced and due only to the order in which the texts were discovered. The ones found later, such as *Hymn to Enlil*, show him in a softer light. However he and his offspring do tend to be associated with storms and war, and he's often represented as a bull.

By contrast Enki, who was in charge of the Abzu – or watery deep – and often represented as a serpent, is associated with kindness and compassion, and also the transfer of civilisation and scientific knowledge to humankind via a set of 'divine rules' known as *me's*. Although there's some consensus that this 'cosmic triad' were probably the most important of all, both Kramer and Thorkild Jacobsen suggest that Ninhursag – possibly as An's incestuous consort – may have been regarded as superior to Enki prior to the Isin-Larsa dynasty *c.* 2000 BCE. Certainly her accepted role as the original prototypical earth-mother and birth goddess is a crucial one. Then, moving on down the generations, Marduk eventually usurped Enlil as the head of the pantheon by the middle Assyro-Babylonian period *c.* 1000 BCE.

This pantheon clearly forms, at least in part, the basis for the subsequent more-celebrated Western pantheons of the Greeks and Romans. For example there's little doubt that Inanna, as the goddess of love, was the role model for Aphrodite and Venus. However any prolonged and detailed attempt to match the pantheons up exactly is almost certainly a misguided and fruitless exercise.

It is also worth noting that, as with other religions and philosophies, genuine human figures could become at least partly deified in the Mesopotamian world. The most concrete example is that of Dumuzi, one of Inanna's many lovers, who appears in the *King List* under the sobriquet 'the shepherd' as the 5th antediluvian patriarch who ruled from Bad-Tibira.[4] Since the subjects of the *King List* were not normally regarded as members of the pantheon, this entry gives him a definite human flavour. However in the many literary texts in which he appears he's quite clearly positioned as a god, and surely therefore merits his place in the pantheon as Inanna's consort in Figure 2. Indeed to his disgust the biblical Ezekiel finds the women of Jerusalem still worshipping him under his later name of Tammuz in the 6th century BCE.[5] Another example is Ziusudra, the hero of the Flood and the equivalent of the biblical Noah. Although he doesn't appear to merit inclusion as a 'great god', the texts clearly state that he was deified, presumably within the more subordinate levels.

So, let's now move on to a consideration of the all-important Mesopotamian literary texts.

3

THE LITERARY TEXTS

If we start with a general introduction to the Mesopotamian literary texts, they can be split into two segments: those written in the Sumerian language, and those in the Akkadian language. Whilst both used cuneiform script, the former were written before the fall of the Sumerian civilisation *c.* 2300 BCE, the latter after. Furthermore, many of the Akkadian texts that we'll discuss are actually copies made in the late Assyro-Babylonian period, for example as housed in the library of Ashurbanipal at Nineveh. Although these date to as late as the first half of the 1st millennium BCE, they're still written in Akkadian, which remained the written and spoken language of trade and diplomacy throughout the Assyro-Babylonian era.

Although a few of the Akkadian texts appear to be almost perfect copies of Sumerian originals, most have no precursor yet discovered. When attempting to trace their origins, the vast majority come under the category of 'mixed heritage', for a variety of reasons. First, many are thought to be older because of their frequent use of Sumerian loan-words. However, as we've already seen, after the fall of Sumerian civilisation its language survived in the fields of learning and culture, playing a similar role to that of Latin after the fall of the Roman Empire, so this can't be regarded as an acid test. Second, many tablets state that they're copies of 'ancient texts', some even using the wording 'based on the Sumerian original'. However as with the Old Testament – much of which is itself an edited version of older texts, including those under discussion here – the problem lies in unravelling the original aspects of documents that have been repeatedly copied and selectively edited over the course of centuries and even millennia. This is especially true if one is attempting to verify elements that might contain a grain of literal truth.

The reasons for this editing are multiple. It may occur to promote a different religious worldview. For example, most non-Hebrew translations of the Bible use the singular term 'God' throughout to support a monotheistic viewpoint – which is fine as a translation of the Hebrew word *Yahweh* or *Jehovah*, but the word *Elohim* that's used repeatedly in the Old Testament actually means 'gods' plural.[1] Alternatively it may be all-too-humanly motivated more by politics and power. For example, the threat of eternal damnation and torment in the fires of hell was clearly introduced into a number of religions, not least Christianity, to ensure the proletariat did as they were told. Examples in Mesopotamia that mix both religious and political elements are the elevation of the Babylonian god Marduk from local to national status in later versions of the *Epic of Creation*, and the elevation of various rulers to 'demi-god' status to entrench the supremacy of particular city-states. Or, more generally, the names of places and people may be altered to make the text more interesting and relevant to contemporary readers, just as one might update an old joke. For all these reasons and more, even in the Early Dynastic and Old Assyro-Babylonian periods multiple copies of texts even dating to the same period can show significant differences – let alone those that stretch across multiple periods.

The only mitigation against this widespread editing was the practice of copying ancient texts in order to form library collections that would preserve and respect Sumerian literary heritage. As far as we know this practice started with Shulgi, a ruler of the 3rd Dynasty of Ur *c.* the 2100 BCE, and continued right through to Ashurbanipal, the Assyrian king whose extension of the Royal Library at Nineveh *c.* 650 BCE provided the many texts first uncovered by Layard. This copying of texts for official libraries involved no political or religious motive to edit and rewrite – rather

THE LITERARY TEXTS

it demanded accuracy and scholarship. This is attested by the fact that professional Assyrian scribes often inserted blanks, their own commentary, or 'I do not understand' in places where their own source tablets were incomplete. But this still doesn't mean we can take these 'official' versions as 'true originals', because of course they may have been copied from previously edited older texts.

Be that as it may, one could suggest that any original Sumerian texts are evidently older and therefore have more potential for factual 'accuracy' – both because they were written closer to the time of the events they describe, and because they'd be less likely to have been subjected to the distortions of the editing process. However there are considerable problems even then. As we've seen the Sumerian written vocabulary is massive, with thousands of words with different signs, and its written grammar is similarly complex.[2] In particular the same written word can have multiple meanings – providing ample chance for punning, a Sumerian favourite; grammatical prefixes and suffixes can be mistaken for word-syllables; the use of tense varies; conjunctions are rarely used; and nouns tend not to have a gender. In addition, their system of writing developed via a number of stages over several millennia.[3] These facts ensure that, even as late as 1987, Thorkild Jacobsen could write in the introduction to his last book of translations:[4]

> It should not be left unsaid, however, that knowledge of Sumerian is still in a rudimentary, experimental stage where scholars differ on essential points, so that translations, even by highly competent scholars, may diverge so much that one would never guess that they rendered the same text. The reasons for this uncertainty are numerous. The writing is in many respects vague and leaves a broad margin for variant interpretation; meanings of words have not yet been exhaustively defined; and – worst of all, perhaps – scholars have not yet been able to agree on basic grammar and its restraints.

Although a number of Sumerian lexicons have now been published,[5] it's therefore undoubtedly the case that the language is so complex that we should be extremely wary of anyone who pretends to be an expert on the subject who is not a dedicated, professional, Sumerian linguist. This contrasts somewhat with the translation of later Akkadian texts. The understanding of the latter is now so advanced that at least two detailed modern dictionaries are available for the professional translator – which leaves considerably less room for debate.[6]

Of course the *style* of writing in all ancient civilisations differs considerably from what we'd use today, reflecting fundamentally different cultures and societies. Consequently certain nuances can only ever be guessed at, and some translations unavoidably appear highly enigmatic if not downright unintelligible. Furthermore the fact that many epics were composed in a poetic style, with much repetition of stanzas and verses so they could be recited to the accompaniment of the lute and harp, doesn't always make for easy reading.

We can deduce that many of the texts recount epic tales that would have originally been preserved and spread by word of mouth over long periods of time. This practice would have continued even after the first written versions had been prepared. This means there are many whole texts, and even more so passages within texts, which evidently come from a common possibly verbal source, but in which details and characters get mixed up and placed in different contexts. So, although we must accept that many Mesopotamian epics are highly literary creations, it's perfectly possible that certain common elements of these traditions carry grains of factual truth.

Related to this, most orthodox commentators tend to use the term *myths*, especially for the Sumerian texts that principally involve deities. In the next chapter I follow this convention to assist the categorisation, but it should be clear that I don't generally support its use, preferring instead the less assumptive word *texts*. This allows us to appreciate that there are undoubtedly some aspects of even the 'mythical' texts that *may* deserve a degree of literal interpretation. Of course, working out *which* aspects is the area of greatest controversy and difficulty.

My own view is that from an esoteric standpoint the multiple references to the 'creation of humankind' and to 'the arts of civilisation being transferred to humankind' are worthy of closer study, while from a more prosaic standpoint I'd say the same of the multiple versions of the Flood story. My reasoning is that these two motifs in particular are mirrored in the sacred literature of other ancient civilisations and cultures from all around the world. The results of my research into these global texts and traditions can be found in Volume 2 of this series, *Atlantis: The Truth*.[7]

When I first came to examine the rich literary inheritance that the Ancient Mesopotamians have bequeathed to us, I found it particularly hard to establish the true extent thereof. Many authors tend to quote the odd major work but it can be difficult for the newcomer to place these in context. I have therefore prepared a proper catalogue of the most important works and the periods in which they were written, one each for the Sumerian and Akkadian texts respectively, in the chapters that follow.

4

THE SUMERIAN TEXTS

The aim of this chapter is to provide an objective summary of the contents of the main Sumerian literary works. Although Samuel Kramer makes a pretty good effort at establishing comprehensive listings, they can be hard to follow and aren't entirely up-to-date.[1] So, by combining the texts described by him *and* by Thorkild Jacobsen I've assembled a list of over 40 major Sumerian literary works – which, perhaps surprisingly, turns out to be around four times larger than the number of their Akkadian counterparts.

    I haven't been able to locate English translations for all the works listed, but those I've used here are primarily taken from Jacobsen's *The Harps that Once... Sumerian Poetry in Translation*. Published in 1987, as far as I'm aware this is the most up-to-date set of translations publicly available without trawling through specialist publications. Only where this anthology omits important works have I then turned to Kramer's earlier *The Sumerians*. This has allowed me to cover all the major texts, and ensured that any summaries and extracts used are the most current and informed available. Furthermore the naming of texts has varied considerably from author to author over the decades, so I've attempted to use full, non-abbreviated versions of the most recent titles alongside alternative or older names, in order to aid recognition when consulting the source works.

    This chapter follows the approach adopted by professional Sumerologists in splitting the literary texts into three categories: myths, epics and divine hymns. The difference between the myths and epics is that the former have gods as their central characters while the latter tend to have mere mortals as their heroes. There are other literary genres – for example royal love songs and hymns, hymns to or laments for temples, admonitory histories, satirical *edubba* texts, debates, proverbs and wisdom literature – but most of these tend to be less interesting for a general audience.

The earliest of these texts date to the Early Dynastic period, that is the middle of the 3rd millennium BCE. However the bulk date to the 3rd Dynasty of Ur and the Isin-Larsa period, that is the late 3rd and early 2nd millennia BCE.

SUMERIAN MYTHS

THE ERIDU GENESIS or THE FLOOD MYTH[2]

One of the most interesting of the Sumerian texts from the point of view of direct biblical parallels, unfortunately this is largely incomplete, with only the bottom third of one six-column tablet so far retrieved – although it's possible to surmise the contents of the missing portions from other similar texts. It dates to the early part of the 2nd millennium BCE, and was excavated at Nippur. It describes the creation of men and other living creatures by An, Enlil, Enki and Ninhursag; the antediluvian cities and their rulers; and the Deluge itself. It is highly likely that this text had a major influence on the equivalent passages in Genesis. Certainly the same narrative is picked up later, albeit with some modification, in the Akkadian epic *Atrahasis*, and also in the introduction to *The Babylonian Chronicle*.

The text opens with Nintu/Ninhursag taking pity on 'her forgotten humankind'. The gods are then described as creating animals the same time as humankind, which is consistent with Genesis but not with most other Mesopotamian creation traditions. The Flood aspect of this text shows typical inconsistencies with other versions too. These include the name of the hero, here Ziusudra – 'the far distant' – of Shuruppak; the length of the Flood – here only seven days and nights; the location in which the boat or ark comes to rest – which here remains unspecified; and whether or not the hero is deified and granted everlasting life – here he is.

MESOPOTAMIA: THE TRUTH

ENKI AND NINMAH/NINHURSAG or THE BIRTH OF MAN[3]

There can be little doubt that this text originally comprised two separate traditions. The first deals with how Enki and his mother Namma create humankind 'from the clay of the Abzu' as slaves, this after the gods had rebelled against their heavy workload, particularly in clearing the irrigation channels on which the area was so dependent. The second describes how Enki and Ninhursag test each other by performing experiments in which deformed or disabled humans are created, for whom the other must find work.

This combination of what had been two texts leads to a number of inconsistencies. First, the juxtaposition of Namma and Ninhursag in the role of 'birth goddess' between the two parts, although Ninhursag does assist in the first part and she definitively the one normally credited with this role. Second, the party at which Enki and Ninhursag test each other 'having drunk beer' is presented in the combined text as a celebration of the initial creation of man. However various references to their disabled creations being put to work in the courts of various kings suggests that humankind must already have been in existence. These inconsistencies are a regular feature of Sumerian poetry in which the integration of originally separate texts often appears somewhat careless.

Orthodox opinion suggests that this text can be interpreted as a polemic on two fronts. First, since the being created by Enki to test Ninhursag is revealed to be deformed only because it wasn't created by a full union between male and female and was somehow 'aborted', it can be seen as a study of the importance of man as well as woman in the reproduction process. Second, it clearly champions the rights of the disabled and can be seen as an early form of political correctness. However in the next chapter we'll see that in the later and more complete Akkadian 'creation of man' texts, that is *Atrahasis*, the *Epic of Creation* and the *Epic of Gilgamesh*, a more esoteric interpretation can be argued to be appropriate.

ENKI AND NINKI/NINHURSAG or A SUMERIAN PARADISE MYTH[4]

This tale is once again clearly made up of two parts that have been merged, with similarly minimal effort at continuity. The entire piece in its present form was undoubtedly written to entertain visitors from the trading centre of Dilmun (identified usually, and definitely here, with Bahrein). The first part especially records how the island was provided with its fresh waters by Enki at the request of his consort Ninki, who is presented here as both his spouse and his daughter – although as we've seen this isn't rare for a Sumerian deity. This allowed it to become a rich and verdant land, with a fine harbour to support its excellent trading connections.

The second part abruptly takes us back to the marshlands of lower Mesopotamia, and begins with Enki attempting to copulate with, this time, Ninhursag – which she only allows him to do once he accepts her as his spouse. There then follows a series of conquests in which Enki ravishes four successive generations of daughters sired by him, and it must be said that his 'I must have that' behaviour is reminiscent of a child in a sweetshop – which, if we accept that the Sumerians didn't find incest distasteful, has the comic effect desired by the author. When he takes the final daughter, Uttu, with some force, her cries are heard by Ninhursag to whom, already tired of her husband's philandering, this is the last straw. She removes Enki's seed from Uttu's body, buries it in earth and eight new plants grow up. Enki, once more the curious child who must try everything, eats them and falls dangerously ill, at which point Ninhursag curses him and vows to never set eyes on him again. A fox comes to his aid and is dispatched to fetch Ninhursag, who accepts his pleas and has the curse removed by the Anunnaki in Nippur. She hurries on to Enki and, after she places him in her vulva, cures each of the eight parts of his body that are troubling him by giving birth to a deity therefrom.

The multitude of confusion of deities and their identities in this text is typical of the problems already discussed, engendered by the tendency of the gods to have multiple liaisons, especially with members of their own family across generations, and of the scribes to alter their roles and names over the centuries – even to the extent of adjusting syllables to make plays on words.

The only real link in these two traditions is that Enki is the main character in both, and even then Jacobsen argues that he may not have been the original subject of the first part. Nevertheless in his much earlier work Kramer takes the analysis further and links the combined text to the biblical 'Garden of Eden' story, on three counts.[5] First, he emphasises the description in the first part of the 'paradise' created by Enki in Dilmun. Second, he likens Enki's eating of the new plants to Adam and Eve's eating of the forbidden fruit of the tree of knowledge. Third, he suggests that the name of the seventh deity engendered by Ninhursag, in this case from Enki's rib and called Ninti, can be translated both as 'lady of the rib' and as 'lady who makes live' – and argues that this is the source of the curiosity of Eve being created from Adam's rib.

On the other hand one might propose that the highlighting of eight different parts of Enki's body that need curing has parallels with the Egyptian myth of Osiris being dismembered by his brother Seth and then reintegrated by his consort Isis. In any case again a more esoteric explanation may be appropriate for elements of this text.

INANNA AND ENKI or THE TRANSFER OF THE ARTS OF CIVILISATION FROM ERIDU TO URUK[6]

Although I've found no original translation of this text, Kramer does provide an outline of its contents. Inanna, acting in her role as tutelary goddess of Erech – later known as Uruk – wishes to enhance her city's reputation as the centre of Sumerian civilisation. She decides that the answer is for her to obtain, by fair means or foul, the 'me's' – see below – that are guarded by Enki in his city of Eridu. This turns out to be rather easy, since they get drunk together and Enki – here described as her father, but we may assume this is poetic licence – simply hands them over. When he sobers up and realises they're gone he's distraught, and dispatches his messenger and a group of sea monsters to intercept and retrieve Inanna's 'boat of heaven' at the first of the seven stopping points between Eridu and Uruk. However Inanna's vizier prevents the capture on this occasion, and then repeatedly thereafter, until eventually she triumphantly reaches Uruk with her prize.

Given their metaphysical nature no clear translation of the word *me's* is likely to be achieved. Kramer calls them 'divine laws', and in the title of the text they're 'the arts of civilisation'. We should also recall that Enki is notorious as the deity who introduced civilisation to humankind, a theme replicated in many other texts from around the world. Fortunately in this text the scribe lists of the order of a hundred me's and, although only 64 are intelligible, this still gives us some sort of idea of what they were. Accepting that the words are often obscure and sometimes untranslatable, Kramer's attempted interpretation of the list is as follows:[7]

> 1: *en*-ship 2: godship 3: the exalted and enduring crown 4: the throne of kingship 5: the exalted sceptre 6: the royal insignia 7: the exalted shrine 8: shepherdship 9: kingship 10: lasting ladyship 11: [the priestly office] 'divine lady' 12: [the priestly office] *ishib* 13: [the priestly office] *lumah* 14: [the priestly office] *guda* 15: truth 16: descent into the netherworld 17: ascent from the netherworld 18: [the eunuch] *kurgarra* 19: [the eunuch] *girbadara* 20: [the eunuch] *sagursag* 21: the [battle] standard 22: the flood 23: weapons (?) 24: sexual intercourse 25: prostitution 26: law [?] 27: libel [?] 28: art 29: the cult chamber 30: 'hierodule of heaven' 31: [the musical instrument] *gusilim* 32: music 33: eldership 34: heroship 35: power 36: enmity 37: straightforwardness 38: the destruction of cities 39: lamentation 40: rejoicing of the heart 41: falsehood 42: art of metalworking ... [43 to 46 missing] ... 47: scribeship 48: craft of the smith 49: craft of the leather worker 50: craft of the builder 51: craft of the basket weaver 52: wisdom 53: attention 54: holy purification 55: fear 56: terror 57: strife 58: peace 59: weariness 60: victory 61: counsel 62: the troubled heart 63: judgement 64: decision 65: [the musical instrument] *lilis* 66: [the musical instrument] *ub* 67: [the musical instrument] *mesi* 68: [the musical instrument] *ala*.

Kramer adds that these 'laws' consist of 'various institutions, priestly offices, ritualistic paraphernalia, mental and emotional attitudes, and sundry beliefs and dogmas'. It is also clear that they include both positive and negative, and quite prosaic, aspects of life.

ENKI AND THE WORLD ORDER: THE ORGANISATION OF EARTH AND ITS CULTURAL PROCESSES[8]

Although the title of this text, translated by Kramer, makes it sound similar to the last one, it actually isn't. After much introductory self-praise by Enki, it describes how he blesses the various lands in and surrounding Mesopotamia with their respective natural resources, and how he ensures their fertility and productivity by appointing gods to look after the various aspects. At the end Inanna complains she hasn't been allocated any real responsibility, but is then pacified by Enki.

This text is interesting from two aspects. First it too contains references to the me's. Second, and more generally, it's clear that it was primarily written to clarify the roles of the various gods in ensuring agricultural prosperity. As such it tends to support the orthodox view that the gods were created by the Sumerians as simple constructs that controlled the varying natural phenomena, including weather, climatic conditions and natural resources – which were evidently outside of their own human control, but incredibly important to the quality of their lives. However, just because one text is clearly written from this relatively prosaic, 'mythopoetic' perspective, it doesn't invalidate the possibility of different, more esoteric contexts being used in other related, and perhaps originally far older, traditions.

INANNA'S DESCENT TO THE NETHERWORLD[9]

The Sumerian version of this text again forms two distinct parts, although on this occasion their merging is more accomplished. The first relates how Inanna attempts to usurp the rule of the netherworld from her sister Ereshkigal. The second contains elements of separate Dumuzi stories, telling of his capture and recapture by a detachment of military police. This comes after Inanna, in a jealous rage, had handed him over to act as a substitute for her in the netherworld, as a condition of her own release.

DUMUZI TEXTS[10]

There are a large number of texts dealing with Dumuzi, who was often referred to as 'the shepherd', many of which again involve his consort Inanna. Their titles used by scholars appear to be more than usually inconsistent, but they include stories about their courtship, their marriage, Dumuzi's unfaithfulness, his dream of death and his actual death. In the main these texts touchingly describe many of the joys and pitfalls of love with which we're all familiar.

ENLIL AND NINLIL or THE BIRTH OF THE MOON GOD[11]

This text describes how Enlil met and wooed Ninlil in Nippur, there union engendering the Moon god Suen – also known as Sin or Nanna. Enlil is then banished from the city by a council of gods because he's deemed to have raped Ninlil. There follow three instances of somewhat confusing trickery in which she's apparently persuaded to sleep with three different people, each of whom are under Enlil's instruction – although in the dark they're replaced each time by Enlil himself. In this way three further sons are born to the pair.

THE NINURTA MYTH or LUGAL-E, THE DEEDS AND EXPLOITS OF NINURTA[12]

Yet again we find this text composed of originally separate traditions, this time three. Part one describes Ninurta's battle with an uncertain 'creature' called Azag that rules the mountains. It is referred to throughout as an object, not a person or animal, and although Jacobsen uses a number of references in the text to argue that it's a plant or tree of some sort, his logic is perhaps not entirely convincing. Similarly enigmatic is Ninurta's weapon, called Sharur, which despite being an object speaks to him throughout and acts as a trusted friend. The gist of the story is that in his familiar guise of 'storm-god' Ninurta launches a pre-emptive strike against Azag, contrary to wise Sharur's advice, which threatens to end in defeat when Azag sends up a dust cloud that blinds Ninurta and his troops. Sharur seeks Enlil's help to extract his son, victory is achieved and Azag is dismembered.

Parts two and three have an entirely different feel, clearly adopting a more mythopoetic style in attributing various natural occurrences to Ninurta's handiwork. On the one hand he facilitates the proper irrigation of the plain by ensuring that the waters of the mountains successfully flow down, and on the other he assigns various practical roles to the 'stones' that acted as Azag's leading soldiers in the battle – good or bad according to the vehemence with which each fought against him.

What can we draw from this? First, it clearly demonstrates the extent to which combination and editing of earlier texts can cause nightmares for attempts at interpretation. For example, it may be that in original versions of the battle story Azag's followers were not stones at all but something else – but the author has inserted them because it fits in with the final story of assigning roles to them. This in turn makes it difficult to shed light on who or what Azag is supposed to be.

Indeed more generally both Kramer and Jacobsen suggest that some of these traditions had been around for so long that, by the time the versions we're studying were being written, the original context was entirely forgotten. In many cases it's possible to argue that this is of no great significance for the work in hand, but there are a few – and I'd regard this as a good example – where this factor *could* play a vital role. Time and again in this text and others we come across sections that could easily be describing the devastation wrought by, for example, a comet impact or major volcanic activity. The problem lies in evaluating how well this interpretation fits the overall context, given the editing process – and the fact that the scribes may have been describing something from long ago that they'd never witnessed, and that they didn't fully understand.

OTHER MYTHS

Kramer lists a number of other myths for which neither he nor Jacobsen provides a translation.[13] These are *Enki and Eridu*; *Inanna and the Subjugation of Mount Ebih*; *Inanna and Shukalletuda: the Gardener's Mortal Sin*; *Inanna and Bilulu*; *Enlil and the Creation of the Pickaxe*; the *Return of Ninurta to Nippur*; and the *Journey of Nanna to Nippur*.

SUMERIAN EPICS

All the major works classed as epics that have been recovered to date involve three rulers from the 1st Dynasty of Uruk c. 2750-2660 BCE, all of whom are listed in the *King List*. They are, in chronological order of reign, Enmerkar, Lugalbanda and Gilgamesh.[14]

ENMERKAR AND THE LORD OF ARATTA[15]

This epic deals with the feud between Enmerkar and an anonymous ruler of neighbouring Aratta, located in the mountains to the east of Uruk – and in modern terms placed by Kramer in North-Western Iran, in the vicinity of lake Urmia and the Caspian Sea.[16] Both men are described as spouses of Inanna, which was the norm for any ruler of a city of which she was the patron goddess, but the tale recounts that she loved Enmerkar best. For his part he was anxious that her temple in Uruk should be of the highest quality, and accordingly he beseeched her to forsake her husband in Aratta, and by blighting his city with drought force him into subservience to Uruk. The 'corvée' work traditionally due to the conqueror would then involve the subjugated Arattans transporting to Uruk the stone and precious metals and minerals that Aratta had in abundance – unlike the Sumerian plain – and building a new temple.

Inanna agrees to the plan, and with military means ruled out by the relatively impregnable location of Aratta, the remainder of the tale is a lengthy account of the trial of wits between the two rulers, both anxious to prove their superiority in protecting their citizens. After a good deal of inventiveness, resourcefulness and wisdom is displayed on both sides, the situation is eventually resolved in an amicable solution in which there's agreement to trade grain and livestock for the required building materials.

This essentially moral tale has one particularly interesting aspect in that it includes a passage that parallels the biblical Babel story, which we'll discuss separately below.

ENMERKAR AND ENSUKUSHSIRANNA[17]

This epic is reviewed briefly by Kramer although I've been unable to locate a translation. It is similar to the last one in that again it finds Enmerkar in conflict with Aratta, but this time with a different ruler.

LUGALBANDA EPICS[18]

According to Jacobsen there appear to be three epics involving Lugalbanda. The first and second once again involve Enmerkar's campaigns against Aratta, and in these Lugalbanda is merely an officer in the army. Given that he's not mentioned as Enmerkar's son in the *King List*, we might assume that it was his very bravery in the campaigns that subsequently bestowed the succession on him.

The first of his epics, *Lugalbanda in the Mountain Cave* – or *Lugalbanda and Mount Hurrum* per Kramer – describes how he and his brothers lead Enmerkar's army across the mountains to subdue Aratta, and how he falls ill on the way, forcing his brothers to leave him in a cave with plentiful provisions. I have however located no full translation of this text.

The second, *Lugalbanda and the Thunderbird* – or *Lugalbanda and Enmerkar* per Kramer – follows on from the first. Having recovered, he roams the mountains aimlessly trying to find his way to Aratta when he comes across the nest of the mighty Thunderbird, which is endowed with magical powers. After caring for its young he's granted a wish on the Thunderbird's return and – given that this version of the story appears to have been written to entertain visiting envoys and messengers – he requests and is given speed and endurance. He rejoins the army, much to his comrades' surprise after he'd been given up for dead, but the campaign is not going well. Enmerkar wishes to get a message back to Inanna in Uruk, requesting permission to call off the siege, but can find no envoy to cross the dangerous mountains until Lugalbanda volunteers. His new gifts allow him to make the journey easily, and on arrival Inanna tells him of an obscure way to defeat Aratta that involves the capture and eating of a special fish. Thereafter the text becomes highly fragmented. The main point of interest here, apart from the adding of substance to the Enmerkar epics, is the Thunderbird itself. It is somewhat enigmatic, and it's not easy to interpret what it might represent – although of course it may be that it's nothing more than a mythopoetic invention.

The third epic, *Lugalbanda and Ninsun*, tells how he married his goddess wife in the eastern mountains and brought her back to Uruk. Again I've been unable to locate a full translation of this text.

GILGAMESH EPICS

Kramer lists five epics in which Gilgamesh, the most famous of the Sumerian heroes, is the central figure.[19] Also known as Izdubar, he's regarded by some as the role-model for the epic heroes of many other cultures. Some other Sumerian texts refer to him as fully deified, while others still see him at least semi-deified, on account of his mother being the deity Ninsun. Given that the *King List* refers to his father as an anonymous 'nomad', and that Lugalbanda comes two before him in the list, Lugalbanda may perhaps be regarded as his adopted father. Certainly if Gilgamesh took over as ruler of Uruk as an outsider, he might well have followed the custom of selecting an illustrious former ruler to refer to as his father.

The bulk of the Sumerian Gilgamesh tablets were found at Nippur, Kish and Ur, and for two of the five epics, *Gilgamesh and the Bull of Heaven* and the *Death of Gilgamesh*, those found to date are so fragmented that Kramer provides no further details of their content. The other three are though translated by him, and are dealt with in turn below.

GILGAMESH AND THE LAND OF THE LIVING[20]

This epic provides the origin of two hugely popular themes that are found in similar form all over the world. First the 'George and the Dragon' style tale in which our hero takes on and, with the help of his trusty friend Enkidu, slays the fearsome Huwawa – although the latter's somewhat enigmatic role is to 'protect the land', and at the end Enlil rages about its slaughter. Second it involves the heroic search for immortality. So early on Gilgamesh laments to Utu about 'man perishing' and 'dead bodies floating in the river's waters, as for me, I too will be served thus'. He also wishes to 'raise up a name' for himself while still alive by building a monument using the cedar from the 'land of the living'.

The story is fleshed out considerably in Tablets II to V of the composite and far more complete Akkadian *Epic of Gilgamesh*, which we'll discuss in the next chapter.

GILGAMESH, ENKIDU AND THE NETHERWORLD[21]

This epic is split into several parts. The introduction deals with a highly abbreviated and therefore not particularly instructive version of the creation. This is followed by a description of a tree cultivated by Inanna that turns out to harbour various demons which Gilgamesh routs for her. She in turn makes a 'pukku' and a 'mikku' for him from the wood, which Kramer suggests are a form of drum and drumstick. The final part deals with them falling into the netherworld and Enkidu's attempts to retrieve them, which as we'll see is incorporated almost verbatim into Tablet XII of the Akkadian *Epic of Gilgamesh*.

GILGAMESH AND AKA OF KISH

Both Kramer and Jacobsen provide a translation of this relatively short epic.[22] It finds Gilgamesh installed as ruler of Uruk, which at this time is subjugated to the city-state of Kish and its ruler Aka or Agga. Gilgamesh resents this overlordship, engages Aka and his troops when they besiege Uruk, and is eventually victorious with the help of his warrior friend Enkidu. But we can infer that other epics not yet discovered describe how Aka had at one time given shelter to Gilgamesh in Kish – and this tale ends with the latter swearing allegiance to the former despite his victory, so as not to be ungrateful for past favours. In effect he's acted so as to restore his pride but at the same time to maintain his integrity. Accordingly this text can be regarded as an essentially moral as well as a historiographical one, which unusually involves no deities at all. Perhaps because of this distinction it's the only Sumerian Gilgamesh story that's not incorporated in any way into the later Akkadian *Epic of Gilgamesh*.

THE SUMERIAN TEXTS

SUMERIAN DIVINE HYMNS

HYMN TO ENLIL[23]

As we might expect this hymn is one of unreserved praise for Enlil. It describes him as the leader of all the gods, and a benefactor to humankind with superhuman and all-embracing powers, without which nothing could take place. It is also noteworthy for describing how he chose the city of Nippur as his abode, and how his temple – the Ekur, translated by orthodox scholars as 'mountain house' – was built in the sacred region of the 'Duranki', translated as 'bond heaven-earth'. Enlil himself is also described repeatedly as 'great mountain', an epithet whose origins Jacobsen admits are unknown.

HYMN TO INANNA AS WARRIOR, STAR AND BRIDE[24]

This represents a compilation by Jacobsen of hymns to Inanna that appear to have previously been separate texts. Its various parts celebrate her in her different guises: as the goddess of war; as Venus, the morning and evening star; and as the goddess of love, here represented by her acting as a bride. Kramer mentions another *Hymn to Inanna* written by Enheduanna, daughter of Sargon the Great of Akkad, but I can't be certain whether or not this is included in Jacobsen's compilation.

OTHER DIVINE HYMNS[25]

Kramer lists a number of other divine hymns for which neither he nor Jacobsen provide a translation: these are *Hymn to Nanshe*, *Hymn to Ninurta*; *Hymn to Utu*; *Hymn to Nungal*, the daughter of Ereshkigal; *Hymn to Hendursag*, Nanshe's vizier; *Hymn to Ninisinna*, 'the great physician of the black-headed ones'; *Hymn to Ninkasi* goddess of drink; and *Hymn to Nidaba*, goddess of writing, accounting and wisdom.

MISCELLANEOUS SUMERIAN TEXTS

THE BABEL STORY

While reading George Smith's *Chaldean Genesis* I came across a reference to a fragmented Assyrian tablet that supposedly mirrored the biblical 'confusion of tongues' story of Babel.[26] Smith himself doesn't elaborate further, and I can find no other reference to it as a separate text – except in as much as there's an interesting passage in the above-mentioned epic *Enmerkar and the Lord of Aratta* referred to as 'Enki's spell'. Jacobsen suggests this is an abbreviated version of a probably separate and independent myth that was gratuitously grafted into this epic but appears somewhat out of context.[27] In any case the passage clearly describes how at one time humankind could 'address Enlil in a single tongue', but that for an undisclosed reason Enki 'estranged the tongues in their mouths'.[28] Jacobsen suggests that, since Enki is regarded as a protector of humankind, this act must have been intended to placate his brother Enlil – perhaps the implication being that the unilingual prayers and appeals to him by a proliferating humankind were becoming too much for him to bear. In this respect we find parallels in the Akkadian text *Atrahasis* in which, as we'll see, the ever-increasing 'noise of humankind' so exasperates Enlil that he sends the Deluge in order to get some peace.

For what it's worth Smith and other scholars suggest two possible locations for the Tower of Babel if it did indeed exist. One is Birs Nimrud near Babylon, where a seven-stage, 154-foot-high tower has been excavated. The other is the Temple of Bel in the ruins of Babylon itself.

THE GUDEA TEMPLE INSCRIPTIONS[29]

This text is known to be comprised of three cylinders although the first, 'cylinder X', has never been recovered, leaving only cylinders A and B. Written around the time of the Gutian invasion that ended the Dynasty of Akkad, it deals with the building of a new temple by the ruler of Lagash *c.* 2125 BCE. The temple, called Eninnu, is in fact a reworking of an earlier structure and is situated in the capital of the region, Girsu. It describes in great detail the traditional processes for such an undertaking: how permission must initially be granted by Enlil; how the ensi is then commissioned to build it by the patron god of the city, in this case Ninurta; how the temple is designed, built and administered; and finally how Gudea hosts a housewarming party for Ninurta and his guests, the great gods themselves, including An, Enlil, Enki and Ninhursag.

THE CURSING OF AKKAD: THE EKUR AVENGED[30]

This text records how Naram-Sin, the 4th ruler of the Dynasty of Akkad *c.* 2250 BCE, attempts to rebuild the Enlil's temple in Nippur, called the Ekur, without permission – that is, without going through the proper channels as described above. His actions in demolishing it without respect, and in uncovering its most secret chambers, desecrate it to such an extent that Enlil is enraged. He sends the barbarous Gutians from the east to attack and invade the whole area, while in sympathy the other great gods visit devastation on Akkad, the capital city. This then attempts to explain how the supremacy of this short-lived dynasty was cut short.

ROYAL LOVE SONGS[31]

On a more light-hearted note, Jacobsen includes a collection of seven royal love songs penned mainly for Shu-Suen/Shu-Sin, the fourth ruler of the 3rd Dynasty of Ur *c.* 2030 BCE. While they contain little of real significance, their often bawdy nature does serve to remind us that the Sumerians certainly didn't devote all their time to worship of their deities and other lofty matters – indeed they were just as preoccupied with sex as any other society, ancient or modern. Two of these in particular, *My Wool being Lettuce* – wool being a metaphor for pubic hair – and *Vigorously he Sprouted*, are in fact downright crude.

5

THE AKKADIAN TEXTS

As we saw in the last chapter it's far easier to summarise the major Akkadian literary works because there are far fewer – although three of them are by far the best known of all Mesopotamian texts. Once again I've used the most up-to-date translations of which I'm aware, this time prepared by Stephanie Dalley – a fellow in Assyriology at Oxford – in her *Myths from Mesopotamia*, published in 1989.[1] Although she herself admits that her compilation by no means contains the totality of Akkadian literary works, it does undoubtedly cover all the major ones. Almost all of these contain something of interest, so eight of them are described below. The only two exceptions that don't merit this treatment are the *Descent of Ishtar/Inanna to the Underworld*, which we covered sufficiently in the last chapter, and the *Theogony of Dunnu*.

Unlike with the Sumerian texts, scholars don't tend to make a distinction between Akkadian myths and epics. Nevertheless I've made the distinction myself in this chapter, based on the same guidelines that the former are primarily about gods, while the latter mainly involve a human hero – even if said hero is subsequently deified. Once again I've primarily used the Sumerian versions of the names of gods, kings and heroes where appropriate for consistency and ease of recognition – even though those used in Dalley's translations of these texts are naturally the Akkadian ones. Finally the longer texts consist of multiple tablets, and my summaries therefore tend to describe the contents of each.

THE AKKADIAN TEXTS

AKKADIAN MYTHS

THE EPIC OF CREATION or ENUMA ELISH or WHEN ON HIGH

This work consists of seven tablets comprising a total of just over one thousand lines. Multiple copies have been found at Nineveh, Kish and Ashur, all of which date to the first half of the 1st millennium BCE, and all of which have relatively consistent renderings – except that in the version found at Ashur the god of the same name is the central character, rather than Marduk as in all the others. This relative consistency can be partly ascribed to the fact that this text was undoubtedly recited by priests as part of the Babylonian New Year Festival.

Although we've already noted that Marduk is a relative latecomer into the gods' pantheon, his appearance must date the original composition to the first half of the 2nd millennium BCE and the first emergence of Babylon as the centre of power in the region. The fact that all tablets found to date are copies of an older work is attested by their colophons. Furthermore there are some similarities with the Old Babylonian version of the *Epic of Anzu* that we'll come to later – for example, they both contain references to the 'tablet of destinies' and to various enigmatic weapons, including the unidentified 'kasusu-weapon', the 'storm chariot' and the 'flood weapon'. Alexander Heidel even suggests that an older version still must have existed in which Enlil would have played Marduk's role, this analysis being based on the use of Sumerian names for the gods, monsters and winds, but no older original has yet been discovered.

As its modern title suggests, this text describes the Mesopotamian view of the creation of the universe and, more particularly, of Earth and its surroundings. Tablet I describes the creation of the universe by Abzu/Apsu and Tiamat, who in this context are seen by some as the god of fresh water and the goddess of salt water respectively; the creation of the various gods; and how Enki gains control of Abzu and his vizier, Mummu. Tablet II covers the attempt to find someone to fight Tiamat, whereby eventually

Marduk is chosen. Tablet III is effectively a repetition of its predecessor. Tablet IV describes the battle between Marduk and Tiamat, in which he slays her by shooting an arrow that pierces her belly and splits her in two; half of her he destroys and scatters to the winds, and 'half of her he put up to roof the sky'; he then retrieves the 'tablet of destinies'. Tablet V covers Marduk's reception by the rest of the gods, the granting of overall kingship to him, and his plan to establish Babylon, initially as a city of the gods. Tablet VI describes, relatively briefly, the creation of man by Enki from the blood of Kingu, Tiamat's main warrior; and Marduk's assignation of roles to the Anunnaki and Igigi. Finally, the remainder of this tablet and Tablet VII praise Marduk by listing the 50 epithets that support his position as the head of the pantheon.

Although perhaps somewhat distorted by editing, there may well be an esoteric underpinning to the creation of man element of this text, which as I indicated earlier is subjected to closer scrutiny in the relevant companion volume, *Atlantis: The Truth*.

ERRA/NERGAL AND ISHUM

Consisting of five tablets and approximately 750 lines, this text is Late Assyrian, with versions coming from Nineveh, Ashur, Babylon and Ur. There is little variation between them, and no real Sumerian equivalent exists.

It takes the form of a dialogue between the narrator Nergal, a lesser known god called Ishum who acts as his advisor, and Marduk. It appears to be a cautionary tale with little story content. The aggressive Nergal, who is backed by the 'sebitti' or seven gods engendered by An to assist him in battle, engages in a series of mutual threats with a relatively impotent Marduk, each having a relentless desire to gain control over the other. Despite his role as a calming influence on Nergal, under orders Ishum carries out a partial destruction of humankind, although a sizeable remnant is left and Nergal is persuaded to leave them alone.

My own view, not shared by Dalley, is that this tale exhibits broad parallels with the various Flood stories. It certainly deals with a deliberate destruction of humankind, even though here it's only partial and not achieved by flood. Indeed Marduk makes specific reference to sending a Flood in Tablet I. What is more, once again this text contains vivid descriptions of devastation that may or may not hark back to some major catastrophe on Earth.

NERGAL AND ERESHKIGAL

Two versions of this text exist – a short Middle Assyrian one consisting of only 90 lines found at Tell el-Amarna in Egypt, and a longer Late Assyrian one of 750 lines from Uruk. There is again no Sumerian equivalent.

It describes how Ereshkigal, goddess of the netherworld, is unable to attend a major banquet of the gods. Directed by An, she sends her envoy to collect her 'present', but Nergal is disrespectful to him. Supposedly as a punishment Nergal is ordered to visit her in the netherworld twice, but he ravishes her on both occasions and on the second ends up remaining there as her husband.

AKKADIAN EPICS

ATRAHASIS or WHEN GODS INSTEAD OF MEN

This composite text came together into its current form only in the late 1960s after much painstaking work by Wilfred Lambert and Alan Millard. The Old Babylonian version primarily used by Dalley dates to c. 1700 BCE, and consists of three tablets each with four columns on the front and back. The contents of the various Late Assyrian versions found at Nineveh are fairly consistent with this.

This important text contains the fullest Mesopotamian account of the creation of man, and also a reasonable account of the Flood. It undoubtedly has some roots in the equivalent but shorter Sumerian *Flood Myth* and *Birth of Man* texts, albeit with some key differences. The hero in this version, from which the text takes its name, is Atrahasis – meaning 'extra wise'.

Tablet I describes how the lesser gods – here the Igigi – rebel against Enlil for making them do all the work required on Earth, again mainly referring to the clearance of the irrigation channels that were so important to the region. Enlil summons a council of the gods – here referred to as the Anunnaki – and An and Enki arrive. Enlil wants to quash the rebellion by force, but An – or Enki in later versions – points out that their work is indeed too hard. He suggests man should be created as a worker from 'clay' and the 'blood of a god', and a detailed description follows of how he and Ninhursag achieve this using purification rites and multiple birth-goddesses. However Enlil then becomes angry because of the numerous people on Earth and the resultant 'noise of humankind', so a plague is sent on them. Atrahasis is introduced at this point, asking how long it will last.

Tablet II mainly repeats Enlil's complaints and describes the plagues, droughts and famines sent by him – even how after six years of this treatment humankind turns to cannibalism. It then moves on to Enlil's command that a Flood must be sent, and his subsequent argument with Enki, who doesn't agree with the plan to destroy the race he himself has created.

Tablet III begins with Enki instructing Atrahasis to listen to him as he speaks from behind a wall, which is Enki's way of warning him of the Flood to come while ensuring he can't be accused of telling him directly. Enki advises him to build a boat and provides details of its construction and contents, and the ensuing Flood is described in detail. Somewhat late Ninhursag bewails the fate they've decreed for humankind, blaming An for chairing the assembly. Interestingly the gods themselves appear to starve during the seven days and nights of the Flood, which has led some commentators to suggest that the text admits they couldn't actually avert it and only had little forewarning themselves.

Unfortunately a large gap means we have no information about the end of the Flood, or on the location where the boat comes to rest, but Tablet III recommences with Atrahasis cooking food for the hungry gods, its fragrance attracting them to return to Earth. Enlil rages when he discovers that a man has survived, An suggests it was Enki's doing, and the latter – despite his earlier subterfuge – proudly admits that he defied them to save humankind. Missing lines follow, but it appears that Enki placates Enlil, then agrees the destiny of humankind with Ninhursag in the final lines. Unfortunately these are fragmented, but they indicate that one third of humankind should do one thing (unknown), another third should do something else (also unknown), and the final third should be prevented from being able to give birth to act as a control on the population.

There are clearly many important parallels between the creation of man and Flood aspects of this text, not only with various others from Mesopotamia and, for example, the Book of Genesis, but also with other traditions from around the world – all of which I examine in more detail in the relevant companion volume.

THE EPIC OF GILGAMESH

We noted in the last chapter that this Akkadian epic is largely based on a composite of four individual Sumerian texts; also that whilst Tablet XII is reproduced almost verbatim from part of *Gilgamesh, Enkidu and the Netherworld*, the details of the others have been changed, sometimes considerably. It is also clear that Tablet VII has taken some input from the *Descent of Inanna*, and Tablet XI likewise from the *Flood Myth*. In fact this text arguably contains the fullest Mesopotamian account of the Flood story, and follows the earlier version in that the hero Utnapishtim – translated as 'he found everlasting life' – is subsequently deified.

Although the earliest fragments of a composite version of the epic were found at Ur and Sippar, and date to the Old Babylonian period, it appears they may not have included the Prologue, Dreams and Flood elements. The most common composite version, on which we concentrate here, is Late Assyrian and was found at Nineveh. It comprises twelve tablets, with between two and six columns on each.

Tablet I starts by describing Gilgamesh as one who 'gained complete wisdom', 'found out what was secret and uncovered what was hidden', and 'brought back a tale of times before the Flood'. Furthermore he 'inspected the edges of the world', 'kept searching for eternal life' and 'restored to their rightful place cult centres that the Flood had ruined'. He is reported as two-thirds divine because of his mother Ninsun, and as designed with a perfect body by Ninhursag – here Belet-ili. However we gather that he's so ebullient that he annoys his townsfolk, and they plead to the gods for him to be given a companion who will match and occupy him. So Ninhursag – now Aruru – creates Enkidu, who starts off as a primitive, uncivilised man who lives with wild animals. A hunter sees Enkidu by the watering hole and is both scared and annoyed because he has unset all his traps; so the hunter's father advises him to go to Gilgamesh and ask for a young girl to visit, tempt and civilise Enkidu. A somewhat explicit description of the success of this plan follows. Gilgamesh then has a dream that his mother Ninsun interprets to mean that a strong and equal companion will come to join him in Uruk.

Tablet II is heavily fragmented at the beginning and somewhat throughout, but we learn that Enkidu has come to Uruk and won over the young population. He and Gilgamesh have an epic fight, after which they become firm friends. At this point Gilgamesh decides to take on the fearsome Humbaba/Huwawa, 'whose shout is the flood-weapon, whose utterance is fire, and whose breath is death' – and who has been appointed by Enlil to 'guard the pine forest'.

Tablet III is highly fragmented, but sees the elders of Uruk counselling Gilgamesh to take his friend Enkidu to protect and assist him in his fight against Humbaba; reluctantly Ninsun then agrees to the plan.

Tablet IV opens with the two travelling towards the forest. Gilgamesh has three dreams on the way that increasingly frighten him, but Enkidu reassures him they mean that they'll triumph over Humbaba. Enkidu then gets scared himself, and is in turn reassured by Gilgamesh.

Tablet V depicts the epic fight with Humbaba. After receiving assistance from Utu the beast is at their mercy and, despite its pleas for clemency, with Enkidu repeatedly entreating Gilgamesh to finish it off, it's finally killed.

THE AKKADIAN TEXTS

Tablet VI begins with Gilgamesh cleaning himself up after the fight, after which he's approached by Inanna to be his lover. He rejects her after recounting details of how she's destroyed the lives of numerous previous lovers. Furious at this rejection she asks An – here her father – for the 'Bull of Heaven' to kill Gilgamesh. An concedes and Inanna embarks on her destructive path, only to be thwarted by Gilgamesh and Enkidu together slaying the bull.

Tablet VII is fragmented, but appears to describe a dream in which Enkidu learns that a council of the gods has decreed that either he or Gilgamesh must die as a punishment for their slaying of Humbaba and of the Bull, which elaborates on Enlil's furious reaction noted in the Sumerian version earlier. Unfortunately for Enkidu, Enlil decides it will be him. In his rage Enkidu curses the hunter and the girl who civilised him, but Utu calms him, so he cancels his curses and accepts his fate. He proceeds to recite a dream of his imminent journey to the netherworld to Gilgamesh, and grows progressively weaker.

Tablet VIII, again fragmented, sees Gilgamesh reassuring his friend how greatly he'll be missed by animals and humans alike, and arranging for a magnificent statue of him to be built.

Tablet IX opens with Gilgamesh roaming the country in mourning for his friend. He decides to visit Utnapishtim, the deified Flood hero, to obtain the secret of eternal life – in order that he doesn't have to suffer the fate of his friend. He travels to Mount Mashu, from which Utu or the Sun emerges, which is guarded by fearsome scorpion-men. He explains his quest in retracing Utnapishtim's original journey, and is eventually allowed to pass. After travelling through ten leagues of total darkness, he finally emerges into a sunlit place of great beauty.

Tablet X sees him wandering by the sea where he meets a barmaid – literally 'ale-wife' – who lives there. She questions his unkempt and sorrowful appearance, and he tells her of his friend's death and his search for Utnapishtim. She tells him no-one has crossed the lethal waters since time immemorial, except for Utu himself, but nevertheless directs him to the ferryman Urshanabi. For no apparent reason Gilgamesh initially fights the ferryman, but they then converse and again Gilgamesh has to explain his sorry appearance and state of mind. They embark, and with Gilgamesh rowing they reach Utnapishtim – whose dwelling place is unfortunately unclear due to fragmentation. The latter questions Gilgamesh for a third time about his appearance, before suggesting that it's natural for a man to be mortal so he should accept death.

Tablet XI has Gilgamesh starting to pick a fight with Utnapishtim, and asking why he has been allowed to gain immortality even though their appearance is identical. Utnapishtim then recounts his involvement in the Flood in some detail. He describes how Enki spoke to him from behind a wall, and how he filled his boat with the 'seed of all living things'. How the gods made their own escape to heaven, how they suffered themselves, and how they wept at humankind's destruction. How his boat came to rest after seven days and nights on Mount Nimush, and how he released a dove, then a swallow, then finally a raven, none of which returned. How he made offerings that the gods smelt and flocked to, and how Enlil was furious at discovering survivors. How Enki admitted his contrivance, and suggested that in future famine and suchlike would be a fairer way of keeping the population under control. Finally how Enlil then blessed him and his wife, and made them immortal 'as the gods'. Utnapishtim then suggests that if Gilgamesh wants to achieve immortality he must first go without sleep for seven days and nights. Gilgamesh fails this test and leaves. But Utnapishtim is persuaded by his wife to reveal to our hero the whereabouts of the 'tree of life', which he subsequently retrieves from underwater – in fact from the Abzu, Enki's abode. However on his journey home he bathes in a pool, and a snake – a symbol for Enki – steals the plant back. Finally he returns to Uruk empty-handed.

Tablet XII appears out of context because Enkidu reappears apparently alive, and it was probably added on to complete the moral aspects of the tale – although with little regard to continuity. In any case, it begins with Enkidu agreeing to go down into the netherworld to retrieve the 'pukku' and 'mekku' that Gilgamesh has lost.[2] Our hero advises Enkidu that he mustn't be clothed in fine garments or he'll be recognised as a stranger, and that he mustn't kiss the dead members of his family. However Enkidu fails to heed this advice, and is thereby prevented from returning. Gilgamesh requests help from Enlil, Nanna and finally Enki, who tells him to open up a hole in the earth to retrieve the 'spirit' of his friend – in other words, he won't come fully back to life. They are reunited, and Gilgamesh urges Enkidu to tell him about the netherworld. Although initially the latter tells him this would be dangerous, he then reveals the condition of various people our hero has known in life. From the descriptions given not everyone appears to be suffering in the netherworld, but some are, and overall it doesn't come across as a particularly inviting place.

This composite text can definitely be regarded as essentially a moral tale. It expresses views about mortality, which is portrayed as humankind's lot; about life after death, where the spirit lives on in the somewhat unwelcoming but relatively bland netherworld; and about how to live life given this state of affairs – the advice effectively being to 'enjoy your life and make the best of it'.

While this epic contains only a few lines dealing with the creation of man – albeit that again they involve Ninhursag, purification and 'clay' – the description of Enkidu as originally a primitive man who cavorted with wild beasts suggests that he represents humankind before its 'civilisation' by the gods. This is again a more esoteric aspects that I discuss in greater detail in the relevant companion volume.

ADAPA

The full length of this fragmented text, which currently stands at about 120 lines, is unknown. The tablets we have were discovered at Tell el-Amarna in Egypt and at Ashur, and date to the second half of the 2nd millennium BCE. To date this text has no real Sumerian equivalent.

Important background information about the central character, Adapa, is known primarily from the work of Berossus – wherein, as

Oannes, he's the first of the antediluvian 'seven sages' sent by Enki from the Abzu to teach the arts of civilisation — or me's — to humankind.[3] We also learn from Tablet II of *Erra and Ishum*, which we'll consider shortly but in which the sages are referred to as 'craftsmen', that Enki banished them back to the Abzu and deprived them of immortality when they angered him. *Adapa* is consistent with this theme in that it opens with him being described as 'extra-wise' — exactly as Atrahasis above — and as 'one of the Anunnaki', who has been given wisdom but not eternal life.

The main part of this short tale is devoted to a description of a visit by Adapa to An in heaven to explain why he 'broke the wing of the south wind'. To prepare him Enki tells him to flatter the gatekeepers, Dumuzi and Ningishzida, by telling them they're sorely missed on Earth now that they've permanently ascended to heaven. He also tells him to avoid the bread and water of death when offered it by An. However the use of a pun means that this can also be interpreted as the bread and water of eternal life, so he ends up being tricked by either Enki or An — which one is unclear — the outcome being that he rejects immortality.[4]

ETANA

This text is again relatively short, and again its full length is unclear due to fragmentation. What we have consists of three tablets and approximately 450 lines. An Old Babylonian version hails from Susa in Elam, a Middle Assyrian one from Ashur, and a Late Assyrian one from Nineveh — this being the version primarily used by Dalley. Again so far no real Sumerian equivalent has been found, but the tale is known to date to at least the middle of the 3rd millennium BCE by virtue of a cylinder seal of that period that unquestionably shows Etana on the back of an eagle.

The *King List* records Etana as the 13th ruler of the 1st dynasty of Kish *c.* 2750 BCE, this being the first post-Flood dynasty. It also describes him as 'the shepherd, he who ascended to heaven, who made firm all the lands'. This description corroborates the story in this text, in which the pious Etana enlists the help of Utu to provide

THE AKKADIAN TEXTS

him with the 'plant of birth' to cure his apparent infertility. He rescues an eagle that has been imprisoned in a pit by Utu after it ate a serpent's offspring, and the eagle takes him towards heaven. However he becomes scared, and they return to Earth. They ascend again after Etana has had various dreams, and finally reach heaven – but the end of the text is incomplete, so we don't find out what happens next.

This text may act as some sort of forerunner to the biblical accounts of Elijah being taken up into heaven in a 'chariot of fire';[5] and of Enoch being given a guided tour of heaven as described in the apocryphal *Book of Enoch*.

THE EPIC OF ANZU/ZU

Two versions of this epic have been found: a shorter Old Babylonian one, and a longer Late Assyrian one from Nineveh. It consists of three four-column tablets and approximately 720 lines. Again there's no real Sumerian equivalent, although Dalley associates Anzu/Zu with the Sumerian Thunderbird in the *Epic of Lugalbanda*. Meanwhile Thorkild Jacobsen draws similar 'lion-headed bird' parallels with Ninurta's weapon Sharur in the *Ninurta Myth*. However both of these are benevolent, whereas here Anzu clearly isn't. Furthermore Sharur is actually mentioned separately in this text, rendering that comparison potentially redundant – indeed it seems more appropriate to draw parallels with Ninurta's old enemy Azag.

In any case it commences with Anzu acting as a trusted servant to Enlil. He then decides to make off with the 'tablet of destinies', which confer the 'Enlil-power' and render him all-powerful and virtually indestructible. After Ishkur, Gibil and Shara have turned away from conflict with him, Ninurta eventually vanquishes him in a terrifying aerial battle.

The enigmatic 'tablet of destinies' – which we previously came across in the *Epic of Creation* – is a difficult concept to interpret, although it's possible that it bears some comparison to the 'divine rules' or me's mentioned repeatedly in Sumerian texts. Meanwhile the 'composite', multi-creature nature of Anzu, and of the various other weapons and creatures that crop up in Mesopotamian texts, perhaps bears some comparison to the composite nature of many Egyptian deities.

PART TWO

ZECHARIA SITCHIN

6

INTRODUCTION

The first of Zecharia Sitchin's *Earth Chronicles* series of books, *The Twelfth Planet*, was published in 1976. Perhaps the most appropriate way of introducing him is to quote from the cover of the 1991 edition:

> Sitchin was raised in Palestine, where he acquired a profound knowledge of modern and ancient Hebrew, other Semitic and European languages, the Old Testament, and the history and archaeology of the Near East. He attended the London School of Economics and Political Science and graduated from the University of London, majoring in economic history. A leading journalist and editor in Israel for many years, he now lives and writes in New York.
>
> One of the few scholars able to read and understand Sumerian, Sitchin has based *The Earth Chronicles*, his recent series of books dealing with Earth's and man's prehistories, on the information and texts written down on clay tablets by the ancient civilisations of the Near East. His books have been widely translated, reprinted in paperback editions, converted to Braille for the blind, and featured on radio and television programmes.

Again quoting from the cover, we'll let Sitchin speak for himself in introducing his books:

> The *Earth Chronicles* series is based on the premise that mythology is not fanciful but the repository of ancient memories; that the Bible ought to be read literally as a historic/scientific document; and that ancient civilisations – older and greater than assumed – were the product of knowledge brought to Earth by the Anunnaki, 'Those

INTRODUCTION

Who from Heaven to Earth Came'.

The *Twelfth Planet*, the first book of the series, presents ancient evidence for the existence of an additional planet in the Solar System: the home planet of the Anunnaki. In confirmation of this evidence, recent data from unmanned spacecraft has led astronomers to actively search for what is being called 'Planet X'.

The subsequent volume, *The Stairway to Heaven*, traces man's unending search for immortality to a spaceport in the Sinai Peninsula and to the Giza Pyramids, which had served as landing beacons for it – refuting the notion that these pyramids were built by human pharaohs. Recently, records by an eye witness to a forgery of an inscription by the pharaoh Khufu inside the Great Pyramid corroborated the book's conclusions.

The Wars of Gods and Men, recounting events closer to our times, concludes that the Sinai spaceport was destroyed 4,000 years ago with nuclear weapons. Photographs of Earth from space clearly show evidence of such an explosion.

Such gratifying corroboration of audacious conclusions has been even swifter for *The Lost Realms*. In the relatively short interval between the completion of the manuscript and its publication, archaeologists, linguists, and other scientists have offered a 'coastal theory' in lieu of the 'frozen trekking' one to account for man's arrival in the Americas – in ships, as this volume has concluded; have 'suddenly discovered 2,000 years of missing civilisation', in the words of a Yale University scholar – confirming this book's conclusion; and are now linking the beginnings of such civilisations to those of the Old World, as Sumerian texts and biblical verses suggest.

I trust that modern science will continue to confirm ancient knowledge.

In fact this description somewhat undersells certain key elements of Sitchin's theories, especially in relation to the contents of *The Twelfth Planet*, his most widely-read and influential book. Not only does this most radical of alternative historians suggest that the aforementioned Anunnaki were a race of 'flesh and blood' gods capable of space flight who visited Earth nearly half a million years ago from a home planet the Ancients called 'Nibiru'. He then goes on to speculate that they came in order to mine precious minerals that were abundant on our planet; that they created modern *Homo sapiens* by genetic engineering, mixing their own genes with those of the primitive hominids they encountered – i.e. 'in their own image'; that they did this in order to create a slave race to take over the mining and refining work; and that they lived for sometimes thousands of years, were capable of good, evil, compassion and brutality, and warred with each other and their human offspring.

Sitchin's comments on how he first embarked on this unorthodox path of research many decades ago are also illuminating:[1]

> My starting point was, going back to my childhood and schooldays, the puzzle of who were the 'Nephilim', that are mentioned in Genesis 6 as the sons of the gods who married the daughters of man in the days before the great flood, the Deluge. The word *Nephilim* is commonly, or used to be, translated 'giants'. And I am sure that you and your readers are familiar with quotes and Sunday preachings, etc., that those were the days when there were giants upon the Earth. I questioned this interpretation as a child at school, and I was reprimanded for it because the teacher said 'You do not question the Bible'. But I did not question the Bible, I questioned an interpretation that seemed inaccurate, because the word *Nephilim*, the name by which those extraordinary beings 'the sons of the gods' were known, means literally 'Those who have come down to Earth from the heavens', from the Hebrew word *nafal* which means to fall, come down, descend.

This experience proved to be the prototype for the major foundation that underpins Sitchin's whole approach: the reinterpretation of key words that appear in ancient texts in various languages. It was this approach, combined with a purported re-evaluation of archaeological and scientific evidence in order to support his theories, that led him to such a startling series of conclusions.

Apart from *The Twelfth Planet*, the full series includes *The Stairway to Heaven* (1980), *The Wars of Gods and Men* (1985), *The Lost Realms* (1990), *Genesis Revisited* (1990) and *When Time Began*

INTRODUCTION

(1993). There is no doubt that their publication has led to Sitchin being feted by many as a visionary and scholar, with a 'guru-rating' that's almost off the scale. Indeed at first sight his knowledge of ancient Near Eastern history and language appears so vast that few authors have even attempted to elaborate on his work, let alone dare to criticise it.

But is everything in the garden as rosy as it appears to his legions of followers? Let us find out...

7

SITCHIN'S SUPPOSED SCHOLARSHIP

I first read *The Twelfth Planet* in the mid-1990s, which was a very early stage in my own research career. I was immediately hooked. It asks seriously provocative questions about every aspect of humanity's development in antiquity, and then provides even more provocative and outrageous answers. There are undoubtedly huge swathes of people who, like me, have long held a general sense that 'there's more to all this than meets they eye'. For me, as with so many others, this was fuelled by reading Erich von Däniken's seminal *Chariots of the Gods* several decades earlier, and it had smouldered ever since. Then I discovered *The Twelfth Planet* and my alternative fire was well and truly lit. The book actually doesn't flow particularly well, but it contains so many seeming gems that one tends to read it in a frenzy of excitement: 'At last, the answers to everything we've been searching for!'

But then I was approached to write a first book about the infamous monuments at Giza in Egypt, and before long I and my co-author Chris Ogilvie-Herald were knee-deep in pyramid research. I began that undertaking with much more of an alternative than an orthodox leaning, not only because of Sitchin but also other alternative authors like Graham Hancock and Robert Bauval, who *seemed* to be equally thorough in their questioning of orthodox opinion. But as *Giza: The Truth* progressed I gradually began to realise how proper research works. You can't just take things at face value. If you're going to have any credibility as an author and researcher you have to do work for yourself, not least in checking what other authors are saying and, wherever possible, going back to the original source of any piece of information to check its authenticity and accuracy. This is, of course, standard research scholarship – although quite how its basic principles had managed to pass me by when studying economics at University College, London, I'm really not sure. Of course most readers don't have time to do such checking – which is why it's so important that someone who does have the time and inclination, like me, *does* do it.

In any case, when I saw copious endnote references and bibliographies in the books by Hancock, Bauval et al, I initially assumed they must be adopting a similarly thorough approach. But that's when I had my first big shock. For whatever reason I needed to check a couple of facts out – and the more I dug, the more I realised that I often couldn't put any reliance on their presentation of supposed 'facts' at all. Now let's be clear that any author, whether in the orthodox or alternative camp or anywhere in-between, will *always* be somewhat selective in how they present their information and arguments. It goes with the territory, however much we pretend to ourselves that we're being as unbiased and neutral as we possible can. That is exactly why there's a complex and thorough system of 'peer review' amongst scholarly communities in all fields of research. But what I increasingly came to realise was that such a process was sadly lacking and sorely needed in the field of alternative history. It became clear to me that there's such a thing as being *unconsciously* selective, and then there's being *deliberately* and *knowingly* selective – to the point of bordering on distortion and, in some cases, even deliberate falsification of evidence. Sadly I found there was a great deal of the latter going on in alternative circles.

This of course meant that at some point I had to go back and re-evaluate Sitchin's work. In fact I'd already had a major alarm bell while researching *Giza: The Truth*. This was when I discovered, as mentioned in the Preface, the entirely unfounded accusation he had made against Colonel Richard Howard Vyse in suggesting he'd faked the 'Khufu quarry marks' in the Relieving Chambers in the Great Pyramid, which provide some of the best evidence for an orthodox date for the monument. If you consult Vyse's extensive original diaries in the British Library, and investigate the quarry marks in situ – as I did – you realise just how profoundly disingenuous Sitchin's accusation was.

So I returned to *The Twelfth Planet* sadder, and considerably wiser. The first thing that hit me now I had some research experience was how, although it contains many apparent in-text references and a reasonable bibliography, there are no proper endnotes at all. This should raise huge alarm bells for anyone who isn't completely inexperienced and naïve in these matters, as I originally was. What is more, many of the more contentious assertions are presented with little or no source information – and this is especially true of his textual 'quotes' from Mesopotamian literature, which are usually his own interpretations and not taken direct from the work of other scholars. This means that merely locating the relevant passages in orthodox translations can require exasperating hours of detective work and, even if you do manage to find them, they often bear little resemblance. Similarly much of his pictorial evidence based on carvings and reliefs on tablets and stelae is in the form of hand-copied drawings – which is fine if they're properly referenced to the original piece in a museum collection or whatever, but often they're not. This makes them similarly exasperating to trace when attempting to ensure they can be relied on as accurate representations of the original.

To be fair and balanced about this, we did see in chapter 3 that even expert Sumerologist Thorkild Jacobsen admitted relatively recently that the study of the Sumerian language, while not exactly in its infancy, still allows professional scholars to produce translations that 'may diverge so much that one would never guess that they rendered the same text'. On the face of it this gives Sitchin *some* potential support. However there are a number of factors that militate against this in his case:

SITCHIN'S SUPPOSED SCHOLARSHIP

1. Even when his 'evidence' comes from Akkadian texts that don't suffer from the same degree of uncertainty, his translations still diverge massively from those of orthodox scholars.
2. On the rare occasions that he does use orthodox translations they're usually regarded as obsolete and, even more important, he can be extremely selective in his extracts. Nowhere is this better demonstrated that in the evidence he uses to suggest that the word *shem*, translated by modern scholars as 'name', derives from a root that he interprets as a 'sky chamber' of some sort. This is such a good example that I've devoted the entirety of the next chapter to a case study thereof, for those who wish to review the detailed support for my criticisms. In my view this case study indicates that, at least in some cases, Sitchin shortens and even omits intervening lines from extracts that, when restored to their full length, render his interpretation meaningless and impossible given the proper context.
3. One professional linguist who did take the trouble to examine Sitchin's work came up with massive criticisms of his understanding of Ancient Mesopotamian languages. These were made anonymously in some newsgroup postings in the early 90s by what turned out to be a professor of Near Eastern Studies at a well-known American University, with whom I had some brief subsequent correspondence.[1] The gist of his criticisms was that Sitchin demonstrates a consistent lack of appreciation of even some of the most basic fundamentals of Sumerian and Akkadian grammar – even to the extent of regularly failing to distinguish between the two entirely different languages, and mixing words from each in interpreting the syllables of longer compound words.

As an example, he analysed Sitchin's interpretation of the name Marduk as 'son of the pure mound'.[2] He suggested that Sitchin had mixed the Akkadian word *maru*, which means 'son', with the Sumerian words *du* and *ku*, meaning 'mound' and 'pure' respectively. But, he asserted, such words from different languages were never mixed, even in a proper name, because the Ancient Mesopotamians only ever used word-combinations taken from one language or the other. Our source provided countless other examples of this type of confusion, for example in Sitchin's translations of shem, mu, naru, Enki, Enlil, Eridu, Ishkur and Tiamat, which seemed to provide compelling evidence that the bulk of his interpretations were spurious and entirely incorrect – apparently made up from bits and pieces of different languages, and with letters and syllables swapped at will. Since these examples all came from just a few chapters of *The Twelfth Planet* – before our source decided he had better things to do with his time – *and* he found hardly any translations that *weren't* distorted, the conclusion he drew was that *none* of Sitchin's translations and interpretations could be implicitly trusted.

4. Another professional linguist has more recently been extremely eloquent and detailed in his condemnation of Sitchin's supposed scholarship and, more important, has openly published his criticisms on his website.[3] Michael Heiser has a PhD in Ancient Semitic languages from the University of Wisconsin-Madison and, among other things, he deconstructs Sitchin's linguistic interpretations of words such as Nibiru, Anunnaki and shem, and the context in which they're used. He concludes: 'I can tell you – and show you – that what Zecharia Sitchin has written about Nibiru, the Anunnaki, the Book of Genesis, the Nephilim and a host of other things has absolutely no basis in the real data of the ancient world.'

5. Even where Sitchin's alternative interpretations might have some degree of foundation, the implications that he derives from them can be highly implausible for other reasons. A prime example of this is his interpretation of the *Epic of*

Creation, in which his argument that this is a literal description of the formation of our solar system is supported by assumptions that, from the perspective of cosmology and astronomy, are highly dubious. Similarly the idea of a 'Planet X' being able to support physical lifeforms when its supposed orbit is so very far from the Sun. Once again these are subjects to which we'll return, this time in chapter 9.

6. He shows a great deal of imagination in weaving the web of a story from all this 'evidence' that, over the course of the entire *Earth Chronicles* series has resulted in a highly detailed account of events on Earth over several hundred thousand years. But in doing so he makes an incalculable number of assumptions, the incorrectness of any one of which would invalidate whole sections of his work. As a case in point, he relies heavily on assumptions about relationships between members of the Sumerian pantheon – for example, repeatedly using the underlying theme of a rivalry between 'Enki-ite' and 'Enlil-ite' clans as an explanation for a whole series of events spanning many millennia. Yet we've seen in a previous chapter that in most cases it's impossible to *definitively* and *consistently* identify the relationships between different members of the pantheon and their offspring and so on because of the extent to which they vary over time in different texts. It is certainly highly dubious to make definitive assumptions about certain gods coming from a particular branch of the family tree.

As a final example of the quality of Sitchin's work *The Twelfth Planet* contains a hand-copied drawing, apparently of a cylinder seal, which is accompanied by the following description:[4]

> That radioactive materials were known and used to treat certain ailments is certainly suggested by a scene of medical treatment depicted on a cylinder seal dating to the very beginning of Sumerian civilisation. It shows, *without question*, a man lying on a special bed; his face is protected by a mask, and he is being subjected to some kind of radiation.

I have taken the trouble to reproduce this drawing in Figure 3. I would have liked to consult the original cylinder seal, or a picture thereof from a reliable, scholarly source – but I couldn't, because of the complete lack of any reference as to the location and source of the original. Be that as it may, what we see in the drawing is surely a perfectly ordinary looking table, a body wearing a mask with a face on each side, and three stylised wavy lines above it that could represent flames or, even more likely, water – which was often depicted in this way. For Sitchin to use the words 'without question' in relation to his extraordinary, dubious and highly subjective interpretation is, *without question*, totally and utterly misleading and unmerited.

Figure 3: Cylinder Seal Drawing from 'The Twelfth Planet'

8

WHAT'S IN A SHEM?

As we saw in the last chapter, one of the claims that's most fundamental to Sitchin's reinterpretations is that the word *shem*, also written as *mu*, which is used repeatedly in both Sumerian and Akkadian texts and normally translated as 'name' or 'reputation' by orthodox scholars, in fact refers to a far older derivation that originally implied some form of 'sky-chamber'. To quote the man himself:[1]

> The Mesopotamian texts that refer to the inner enclosures of temples, or to the heavenly journeys of the gods, or even to instances where mortals ascended to the heavens, employ the Sumerian term *mu* or its Semitic derivatives *shu-mu* ('that which is a *mu*'), *sham* or *shem*. Because the term also connoted 'that by which one is remembered,' the word has come to be taken as meaning 'name.' But the universal application of 'name' to early texts that spoke of an object used in flying has obscured the true meaning of the ancient records.

He goes on to describe how the etymology of the term can be traced from 'sky chamber' to 'name'. He argues that original stone sculptures of gods inside oval rocket-shaped chambers, which were used to venerate them in places remote from their temples, were eventually copied by kings and rulers and their own images placed thereon in order that they could associate themselves with the 'Eternal Abode', and have their 'name' preserved even if they were only mortal. These objects are what we now refer to as stelae. He further examines the words used for such objects in a number of languages, arguing that they all share common connotations of 'fiery stones that rise'.

Mesopotamian scholars have indicated that this analysis is highly misleading because the term *mu* is a Sumerian verbal prefix that doesn't require translation. For once Sitchin admits to being aware of this criticism, and counters that scholars have deliberately invented this grammatical construct precisely because 'they sense that *mu* or *shem* may mean an object not *name*... and have thereby avoided the issue altogether'.[2]

What are we to make of all this? For a start, it's interesting to note how easy it is to add more fuel to the fire to further obscure the picture. For example, Thorkild Jacobsen notes quite independently of this theme that *shem* can also be used to denote a 'tambourine-like drum'.[3] It would surely be perfectly justifiable for me, therefore, to argue that its use as 'name' or 'reputation' developed from association with the concept of 'banging one's own drum'. This example serves to show how the use of words with multiple meanings, especially in the Sumerian language, can allow all manner of interpretations and associations to be made.

Indeed as we've seen this is true of many words on which Sitchin places great emphasis. Accordingly I've chosen *shem* as a case study for evaluating his interpretations, mainly because in this case he backs his argument up with a large number of extracts from texts that apparently support his case. My own approach was to examine these usually condensed extracts and see if his interpretations made sense in the *context* of the originals from which they came.

Of the twelve main textual extracts that Sitchin uses, three are taken from Sumerian texts, four from Akkadian texts and three from the Bible, while I've been unable to trace translations for the remaining two due to the lack of referencing. They are presented in this order below. I have used the following notation in presenting them: words in square brackets represent the original word in the source text; words in upper case are those omitted by Sitchin from the beginning, middle or end of quotes, which can distort the full

WHAT'S IN A SHEM?

context; and the italics are mine, for emphasis. For each extract I've also added my own analysis.

TEXT EXTRACTS

GILGAMESH AND THE LAND OF THE LIVING, LINES 4-7[4]

> 'Enkidu BRICK AND STAMP HAVEN'T YET BROUGHT FORTH THE FATED END,
> I would enter the land, would set up my name [*shem*],
> In its places where names [*shems*] have been raised up, I would raise up my name [*shem*],
> IN ITS PLACES WHERE NAMES [*shems*] HAVEN'T BEEN RAISED UP, I WOULD RAISE UP THE NAMES [*shems*] OF THE GODS.'

Taken from one of the original Sumerian Gilgamesh texts and not the composite Akkadian epic, this first extract finds Sitchin on highly selective form. At least he does for once give us a clue by providing an ellipsis to indicate that something has been left out of the first line, but when the bulk of it is reinstated as above we can immediately see the connection with 'brick and stamp' – that is, monument building and printing, the conventional method of preserving one's name. Then, when we reinstate the last line, it surely appears far more likely that Gilgamesh is being mindful to respect the reputations of the gods rather than deciding when to use his own rocket as against theirs.

HYMN TO INANNA[5]

I can't find this extract *per se* in Jacobsen's composite version of the *Inanna* hymns, but the following is what Sitchin quotes:

> Lady of Heaven:
> She puts on the Garment of Heaven;
> She valiantly ascends towards Heaven.
> Over all the peopled lands she flies in her *mu*.
> Lady, who in her *mu* to the heights of Heaven joyfully wings.
> Over all the resting places she flies in her *mu*.

Nevertheless Jacobsen's version does contain multiple references to Inanna as the Evening and Morning Star (Venus) that involve her 'lighting up', 'stepping up onto' and 'wandering in' the sky. Consequently it's highly likely that Sitchin has provided his own interpretation of one of these passages, which is even more inventive and imaginative than most of his other extracts. Since as so often he provides no reference as to his source, it's impossible to comment further.

GUDEA TEMPLE INSCRIPTIONS

Again the following extract, being so short, is hard to trace in Jacobsen's translation, but this is Sitchin's version:[6]

> Its *mu* shall hug the lands from horizon to horizon.

One passage towards the end of Jacobsen's version reads as follows:[7] 'He (Ninurta) has indeed established your (Gudea's) *name* from the south to the north.' This could be the same passage, but further comment is useless without a proper source reference.

ADAPA, TABLET II, LINES 57-9

In this case Sitchin doesn't quote an extract proper, merely reporting: 'An demanded to know who had provided Adapa with a *shem* with which to reach the heavenly location.'[8] I have found two translations of this text, the first by Alexander Heidel and the second by Stephanie Dalley. In Heidel's version An wants to know why Adapa has been allowed to visit heaven:[9]

> 'Why has Enki revealed to an impure man
> The heart of heaven and earth?
> He has made him strong and has made him a name.'

Meanwhile Dalley's more recent translation is quite different, and doesn't even contain the idea of a reputation or name. Here An asks how Adapa obtained the power to 'stop the south wind':[10]

> 'Why did Enki disclose to wretched humankind
> The ways of heaven and earth,
> Give them a heavy heart?
> It was he who did it!'

WHAT'S IN A SHEM?

We know that significant progress has been made in translating Akkadian script in recent decades, although Heidel might have used an entirely different set of tablets. In either case, neither of these orthodox translations support Sitchin's interpretation in the slightest.

ETANA, TABLET II, LAST COLUMN[11]

This extract sees Etana asking the god Shamash or Utu to help him obtain the 'plant of birth':

> 'O Lord, let the word go forth from your mouth
> And give me the plant of birth,
> Show me the plant of birth!
> Remove my shame and provide me with a son [shem]!'

Sitchin's extract is sufficiently close in this case for it to be clear that the word he suggests is *shem* is translated by Dalley in the original as 'son', which is slightly confusing. Nevertheless, although she doesn't say as much, her translation would appear to use the phrase 'plant of birth' as a sign that Etana is infertile, in which case it would be quite understandable that he'd want to change the situation and establish a lasting *reputation* by way of offspring. Despite the fuss that's sometimes made about Etana's subsequent description of how the Earth gets smaller and smaller as he ascends towards heaven on the back of an eagle, this is a separate part of the text and is, in any case, only common sense. So once again Sitchin's interpretation appears by far the less likely and obvious.

THE EPIC OF ANZU, TABLET I, COLUMN 3[12]

Here, while Enlil is taking a bath, the evil Anzu steals the 'Tablet of Destinies':

> He gained the Tablet of Destinies for himself,
> Took away the Enlil-power. Rites were abandoned,
> Anzu flew off and went into hiding.

Again Sitchin doesn't quote here, simply suggesting that the epic contains the sentence 'Anzu fled in his *mu*.' Yet there is no direct mention of 'name' in Dalley's translation above, so I was left somewhat in the dark — until contacted by a graduate student of Near Eastern Studies at a US university, who had read an initial online version of the paper on which this chapter is based. As with the expert in the last chapter, he too asked to remain anonymous, but his expertise speaks for itself:

> Most recently, I have finished translating the *Anzu Epic*, which Sitchin makes note of in *The Twelfth Planet*. The relevant portion is, as you quoted, when Sitchin says, 'As Zu fled in his *mu* (translated name but indicating a flying machine)'. In looking at the text of the epic, however, I must tell you that the sign *mu* never appears.

He then goes into a detailed deconstruction of the line in the original Akkadian text, indicating that grammatically the words at the end could never be taken to mean the *means* of transport, only the *destination* — and that only someone with a very imperfect understanding of the Akkadian language could make such an elementary mistake.[13] He concludes:

> What distresses me is that Ancient Mesopotamia has a lot to offer modern Western culture, and it's a shame to see it warped like this.

THE EPIC OF CREATION, TABLET VI, LINES 57–62

Dalley's translation reveals how, after Marduk has vanquished Tiamat and asked Enki to create man, Babylon is originally constructed by the Anunnaki themselves:[14]

> 'Create Babylon, whose construction you requested!
> Let its mud bricks be moulded, and build high the shrine!'
> The Anunnaki began shovelling.
> For a whole year they made bricks for it.
> When the second year arrived,
> They had raised the top of Esagila in front of the Abzu.

Meanwhile Sitchin translates the word Babili (Babylon) as 'gateway of the gods' to arrive at the following translation of the first two lines of the same passage:[15]

> Construct the Gateway of the Gods. Let its brickwork be fashioned.
> Its *shem* shall be in the designated place.

WHAT'S IN A SHEM?

He goes on to use the lines that follow to argue that this mirrors the subsequent attempt by humankind to build a stage tower for launching rockets at the same site in the biblical Babel story quoted below. However, once again we can see that the context is far more likely to refer to the mythical original construction of a temple.

GENESIS 6:4[16]

> There were giants in the earth in those days; and also after that, when the sons of God came in unto the daughters of men, and they bare children to them, the same became mighty men which were of old, men of renown [shem].

For once Sitchin's quoting here appears to be perfectly accurate – he could hardly do otherwise with well-known biblical passages – and it must be admitted that this is about the only case where the use of the word *shem* could equally well reflect either his or the orthodox interpretation.

GENESIS 11:2-8[17]

> And it came to pass, as they journeyed from the east, that they found a plane in the land of Shinar; and they dwelt there. And they said to one another, Go to, let us make bricks, and burn them thoroughly. And they had brick for stone, and slime had they for mortar. And they said, Go to, let us build us a city and a tower, whose top may reach unto heaven; and let us make us a name [shem], lest we be scattered abroad upon the face of the whole earth. And the Lord came down to see the city and the tower, which the children of men builded. And the Lord said, Behold, the people is one, and they have all one language; and this they begin to do: and now nothing will be restrained from them, which they have imagined to do. Go to, let us go down, and there confound their language, that they may not understand one another's speech. So the Lord scattered them abroad from thence upon the face of all the earth: and they left off to build the city.

Again there's nothing wrong with Sitchin's quoting here. However he stresses the impact the actions of humankind had on the gods, especially their fear that 'nothing will be restrained from them', and goes on to suggest that the building of a *shem* would have prevented humankind's being 'scattered abroad' because, as their population increased and they spread out, a 'sky-vehicle' would have allowed them to stay in contact with one another. Although there may be enigmatic aspects to the biblical 'Tower of Babel' story, I'd suggest that it's far simpler and more reasonable to suggest, as orthodox scholars do, that humankind might wish to build an impressive *tower* to make a lasting *reputation* for itself.

ISIAH 56:5[18]

> Even unto them will I give in mine house and within my walls a place and a name [*shem*] BETTER THAN OF SONS AND DAUGHTERS: I WILL GIVE THEM AN EVERLASTING NAME [*shem*], THAT SHALL NOT BE CUT OFF.

Sitchin has taken the liberty of foreshortening this lesser-known biblical passage to lose the context. As soon as the remainder of the verse is reinstated, we must ask why anyone would wish to provide a 'space-vehicle' that was 'better than that of sons and daughters'? Unless rampant material one-upmanship had already infiltrated biblical society, his interpretation makes no sense whatever.

UNTRACEABLE PASSAGES

I have been unable to trace translations of the texts from which the final two extracts used by Sitchin are taken. The first, supposedly from a *Hymn to Ishkur*, apparently contains the line:[19] 'Thy *mu* is radiant, it reaches heaven's zenith.' The second, taken from what Sitchin describes loosely as a *Poem to Ninhursag*, supposedly contains detailed descriptions of the Great Pyramid of Giza, including the lines:[20] 'House which is a great landmark for the lofty *shem*', and 'Mother of the *shems* am I.' Unfortunately neither of these texts is mentioned by Kramer, Jacobsen or Dalley in their major works that I've used as my main sources throughout.

CONCLUSION

We can see that much of Sitchin's textual 'evidence' in support of

WHAT'S IN A SHEM?

his claim that the words *shem* and *mu* refer to 'sky-vehicles' is badly referenced and, to say the least, somewhat creatively interpreted. His tendency in certain cases to leave out surrounding lines that would render his interpretations impossible in the context rings alarm bells that should put any reader on their guard. What is far more disturbing is that in many of these cases it couldn't have been anything other than entirely obvious to him, when he selected his abridged extracts, that the original context *couldn't possibly* support his revised interpretation. In which case he was being knowingly and deliberately duplicitous in order to sell his books to the public.

9

SITCHIN'S COSMOLOGY AND 'PLANET X'

We have already seen that Sitchin's starting point is to ask, who were the Nephilim or Anunnaki? Convinced by his investigations into their supposed use of space travel, as discussed in the last chapter, he turns his attention to identifying the planet – not star – from which they came. He examines the evidence for the Mesopotamians having astronomical knowledge far in excess of that attributed to them by orthodox scholars, and then quotes extracts from a number of very early works on Ancient Mesopotamian astronomy and other topics. Using these he suggests that the Mesopotamians considered our solar system to be made up of twelve planets.

Of course this in itself presupposes a number of things. First, not only did they know about Mercury, Venus, Earth, Mars, Jupiter and Saturn, but also about Uranus, Neptune and Pluto, which have only been discovered by modern astronomers in the last 250 years. Second, they counted the Sun and the Moon as 'planets'. Third – and this is of course Sitchin's big reveal – they knew of the existence of an additional *twelfth planet*.

Despite the objections to this theory that are already obvious, he goes on to suggest that it's this very factor that determined the number of 'great gods' in the supreme pantheon, which he regards as being made up of twelve members. Further, he argues that they used this number in a variety of other contexts as a result – for example, dividing the heavens into twelve signs of the zodiac, the year into twelve months, and the day into two sets of twelve hours.[1]

The main piece of pictorial evidence he cites is a six-pointed star surrounded by *eleven* spheres of varying size, which forms a relatively small part of an Akkadian seal. For once this is not a hand-drawn reproduction but a photograph, and surprisingly we're also given a source – it's part of the *Vorderasiatische Abteilung* collection in the State Museum of East Berlin, and we're even given the catalogue number, VA243. However we shouldn't hold our breath. Sitchin goes on to blow up the relevant section in a separate drawing, and compares it to a representation of what our solar system *would* look like if the planets were placed to scale in a circle around the Sun in order of size, rather than in linear fashion as we normally depict them.[2] Some commentators have objected that just on casual perusal the comparison is pretty flawed in terms of the relative sizes and positions of the supposed planets, but this is splitting hairs – after all, we couldn't expect the Ancient Mesopotamians to be incredibly accurate in this endeavour, if it was indeed what they were trying to do. But was it?

This seal has been subjected to considerable analysis by expert Assyriologist Michael Heiser, who we first introduced in chapter 7. In summary he makes the following points:[3]

1. Sitchin completely ignores the broader context of the seal. It contains textual inscriptions on the left and right that describe a worshipper making an offering to a god in regard to the fertility of the crops, and pictorially these two figures dominate the seal.

2. What Sitchin interprets as the Sun in the part of the seal he concentrates on almost certainly isn't the Sun at all but a star. Although similar, the standard symbol for the Sun is a four-pointed star with a circle in the centre and wavy lines emanating from each quadrant, while for a star it's a six, seven or most often eight-pointed star with a central circle and no wavy lines. The latter, with six points, is clearly what's depicted on the seal. These symbols are used consistently

again and again and again, and to confuse them again shows a fundamental lack of understanding of Mesopotamia symbolism.

3. Gods were usually represented with a star somewhere above their head. Sometimes too a star *system* would be represented with multiple dots, most often the Pleiades with seven. Although slightly unusual with eleven, the representation on this seal is therefore almost certainly some sort of star system. The other possibility is that it represents the twelve 'great gods', each as stars, the central, pointed star being An.

4. Perhaps most important of all, whereas Sitchin quotes much older books, Heiser has made the effort to check every single relatively modern work written by specialists in cuneiform astronomical tablets.[4] Enormous amounts of work have been done in this area since the early days, and our modern understanding of Mesopotamian astronomy leaves very little doubt as to their level of knowledge and so on. As a result Heiser feels confident in asserting: 'There is not a single text in the entire corpus... that says the Mesopotamians knew of more than five planets.'

Despite all the foregoing, Sitchin uses this seal as a major foundation for the existence of a twelfth planet; for its position relative to the others – arguing that its orbit brings it between Mars and Jupiter; for its relative size – apparently smaller than Jupiter and Saturn, but significantly larger than Mars and the Earth; and for its role in the creation of Earth, as we'll shortly see. In my view this supposedly major piece of primary evidence is already completely undermined, but for the sake of it let's complete the job we've started and investigate the rest of Sitchin's related arguments.

THE CREATION OF EARTH

Sitchin places a highly literal interpretation on the Akkadian *Epic of Creation*. This is another of the major pieces of evidence that

SITCHIN'S COSMOLOGY AND 'PLANET X'

apparently persuades him that his twelfth planet was primarily referred to as Nibiru, and was the planet from which the Anunnaki came. Ignoring for the moment whether he has any grounds for such a literal interpretation, let's review the principal elements of his analysis.[5] Note that his interpretation often requires the names of gods to be substituted for those of the planets, so these are provided in brackets where appropriate.

In brief, he suggests that originally our solar system consisted of, in order of orbit, the Sun (Abzu), Mercury (Mummu), Venus (Lahamu), Mars (Lahmu), Tiamat (a planet then orbiting in what's now the asteroid belt), Jupiter (Kishar), Saturn (Anshar), Pluto (Gaga, which was then in a closer orbit), Uranus (An) and Neptune (Enki). He argues that the planet Nibiru (Marduk) came from outer space on a retrograde path – that is, moving in the opposite direction from the rest of the planets in our solar system – was attracted by the gravitational pull of the outer planets into an ever tighter orbit around the Sun, caused a variety of initial disruptions, then on its second pass collided with Tiamat, which split into two – one half forming the Earth that proceeded into a tighter orbit inside that of Mars, the other breaking up to form the asteroid belt. The Moon (Kingu), a satellite of Tiamat, was at the same time shunted into an orbit of the Earth – and because it had originally been a planet in its own right before becoming a satellite of Tiamat and then the Earth, the Moon continued to be regarded as a planet afterwards.

There are primarily two angles from which this interpretation should be judged. First, does his interpretation hold up under the scrutiny of modern scientific understanding? Although I'm no cosmologist, my research reveals that there are a number of objections to his theories – much of which is provided in an internet posting by researcher Rob Hafernik, who has a degree in aerospace engineering:[6]

1. It would require an extraordinary series of coincidences for even one of the Earth, Moon, Pluto and Nibiru to stabilise in a different orbit after a collision without additional accelerative

stimuli. It is therefore highly unlikely that they could all benefit from such an unlikely sequence of events.

2. Sitchin's view of gravity and its effects is hopelessly inadequate. For example, he has Nibiru being affected by the pull of Neptune and Uranus, but there's no contra effect on them. Gravity works both ways, especially since Nibiru is supposed to be of similar size to them, and yet their orbits remain to this day more circular than that of the Earth. Similarly, he suggests that the gravitational pull of other planets could cause 'bulges' in Nibiru sufficient to cause satellites to be ripped out of it – which is a simply idiotic view of how interplanetary gravity works.

3. Nibiru had to make at least two orbital passes to tear Tiamat in half – and yet on the second pass it came back in roughly the same orbit, despite all the gravitational interactions it must have suffered on the first pass that should have altered its orbit considerably. From the opposite perspective, one might also ask why Nibiru managed to cause so much devastation on these first two passes, and yet has had no affect whatsoever on its myriad subsequent passes.

4. As a corollary to the above, Sitchin uses another supposed text – which he doesn't name – to suggest that Nibiru's orbital plane is inclined at 30 degrees to the ecliptic.[7] If this is the case, how did it manage to come so close to so many of the planets in our solar system on its first two devastating passes? Or is he suggesting that once more unknown forces caused it to stabilise in this non-aligned orbit thereafter?

5. The idea that the Moon was originally a planet in its own right is not supported by modern discoveries. The latest thinking appears to be that, most likely, it split off from the Earth after the impact of a Mars-sized body.

The second approach is to question the extent to which it's reasonable for Sitchin to even attempt to place a literal interpretation on this most enigmatic of texts. We have already seen that one of the motives of this relatively late Akkadian work is political – that is to elevate the late-emerging Babylonian god Marduk from local to national status. Sitchin himself acknowledges the political influence, but argues that the text has far earlier Sumerian origins, and in this he's supported by many scholars – despite the fact that no Sumerian version has yet been discovered, apart from similarities in isolated passages. What is more the common practice of amalgamating originally separate texts and tacking on new passages is probably at work. So Marduk's establishment of Babylon and the extensive list of his epithets in Tablets V to VII are likely to be late additions, while a brief version of the creation of man story is stuck in the middle of all this. Since Tablets II and III deal mainly with the search for a champion to fight Tiamat – in which role Marduk finally offers himself – this leaves us with the likelihood that it's primarily Tablets I and IV, if any, that reflect important earlier tales.

Tablet IV deals with Marduk's battle with Tiamat, who represents primeval 'watery chaos', in which he splits her in two to create heaven and earth and restore order to the universe. This is clearly a basic creation theme that ties in closely with that of many other ancient civilisations. For example, Alexander Heidel points out that in Egyptian legends 'the air-god Shu separated heaven and earth by lifting the sky-goddess Nut from the earth-god Geb and placing himself between the two', and that Phoenician and Vedic legends both contain the concept of 'the cosmic egg being split to create heaven and earth'.[8] Meanwhile Sitchin is quite right to draw parallels with Genesis 1:6-8:

> And God said, Let there be a firmament in the midst of the water, and let it divide the waters from the waters. And God made the firmament and divided the waters which were under the firmament from the waters which were above the firmament: and it was so. And God called the firmament Heaven.

Sitchin goes on to argue that the Hebrew word *Tehom*, used in Genesis to denote the 'watery deep', stems from the word *Tiamat*; also that the firmament that was called 'heaven' is, in the original

Hebrew, 'rakia', which translates as 'hammered bracelet' and therefore refers to the asteroid belt.[9] However we've already seen that his etymological work is often flawed while, although I haven't undertaken a detailed comparison, the many extracts from the *Epic of Creation* that he quotes are very much his own interpretations, and almost certainly differ substantially from Stephanie Dalley's. Perhaps most important of all there can be little doubt that all these creation of the earth/world/universe texts should be interpreted from an esoteric rather than a literal viewpoint, which of course I do in *Atlantis: The Truth*.[10] All these factors, combined with the blatant cosmological flaws in his theory, are surely more than enough to utterly refute his interpretation of the *Epic of Creation*.

VISITORS FROM ELSEWHERE?

Even if Sitchin's account of the creation of Earth is fatally flawed, is he nevertheless right to assert that the Anunnaki were indeed extraterrestrial visitors? I can find precious little evidence that the Mesopotamian literary texts even mention the planet Nibiru, let alone assert that it's where the Anunnaki originated. In Dalley's translation of the *Epic of Creation* it's directly mentioned only in the brief passage quoted in the next section, while the remaining references are all to Marduk – and it's only Sitchin's creativity that links the two. Nor have I been able to find any reference to Nibiru in any of the other literary texts. With no supporting argument Sitchin suggests that the multiple versions of a 'winged globe', which are indeed found in great numbers on a variety of reliefs from Mesopotamia and elsewhere, represent it.[11] Yet most enlightened commentators recognise this as a universal, esoteric, archetypal symbol. He goes on to suggest that various Babylonian astronomical texts and biblical passages foretell the events that accompany each return of Nibiru.[12] I admit I haven't taken the trouble to consult these, purely because of the evident weaknesses in all the other aspects of his argument.

It is in fact Sitchin's interpretation of the words Nephilim and Anunnaki that appear to provide most support for this assertion.

Starting with the former, in chapter 6 we quoted his argument that the Hebrew word has the Semitic derivative 'nafal' or 'nfl', which he suggests means 'to fall, come down, descend' – and it's quite true that, although some scholars interpret the word *Nephilim* as 'giants', they're also commonly associated with *'fallen* angels'.[13] But, after quoting supposed backing from the 19th century Jewish biblical commentator Malbim, he becomes expanded in his books into 'those who were cast down upon Earth' and 'those who have come down from the Heavens to Earth'.[14]

As for the Sumerian term Anunnaki, he translates this similarly without any detailed explanation. Now, there's no doubt that the word *An* is the name of the chief deity associated with 'heaven' itself, while the word *Ki* does represent the 'earth' (goddess) – often identified with Ninhursag as the archetypal earth mother or birth goddess. However as we've seen this doesn't mean that when they're found in a combined word the component parts can be neatly deconstructed to suit one's purpose. The two attempts at translation of the entire term that I've found are by John Heise, in which he breaks it down as A.nun.nak and translates it as 'the semen/descendants of the monarch (nun)'; and by Thorkild Jacobsen, who translates it similarly as 'the sons of princes'.[15] According to these experts, therefore, An and Ki aren't even separate component parts of the word, let alone having any connotation with falling.

It should also be noted that, while orthodox commentators suggest the alternative term Igigi is of unknown origin and meaning, Sitchin insists it means 'those who observe and see'.[16] This ties in with his theory that they remained in orbit, and is backed up to the extent that the meaning of the Sumerian word *igi* is indeed 'to see'. However this hardly represents overwhelming evidence of visitors from elsewhere.

Sitchin produces a variety of other examples of interpretations of words and reproductions of statues and stelae to support this assertion. They are too numerous to be analysed individually, but suffice to say there's strong reason to believe that, as evidence, they all suffer from the same inadequacies as those we've already considered here and in previous chapters. Yet he does produce one other piece of evidence that at least at first sight appears quite enigmatic, sufficiently so for us to consider it here. It is a most interesting circular clay tablet, around 5.5" in diameter, which was found in the ruins of King Ashurbanipal's library in Nineveh and is now in the British Museum as exhibit K8538 (see Plate 5). Although about 40 per cent of the surface is worn away, it's divided into eight equal triangular segments, and clearly contains an assortment of repeated cuneiform signs along the dividing lines and elsewhere.

Sitchin quotes a number of studies from the turn of the twentieth century in which a consensus developed that it's a planisphere, or map of the night sky. However he reports that these early scholars struggled with the interpretation of what they considered, given its location and age, to be Akkadian cuneiform signs – and that it was only when *he* attempted to read them in Sumerian that they started to reveal a 'Celestial Route Map' that records how the Anunnaki travelled to Earth via the outer planets.

Even if he were right about the language used, based on the fact this is supposedly a copy of an older Sumerian tablet, as usual his interpretations of the words thereon are still open to question. Here are some examples: we have *sham* (not *shem*) translated as 'rocket', an interpretation we've already dismissed in the last chapter; *na* translated as 'high', when the word *an* is the normal Sumerian term for this because of the association with An; and *apin* translated as 'where the right course is set', when every use of the word that I can find clearly indicates it means 'plough'.

Sitchin's further interpretation of this tablet is a hotchpotch of ideas that mixes, for example, supposedly technical flight direction details with mundane issues such as stocking up with grain for the return journey. Is it really likely that the two would be combined on one diagram of such supposed importance? Furthermore we might question how such a technical set of instructions could sensibly be expressed using such unspecific terms as 'high', 'sky', 'mountain' and so on, which he says are used repeatedly.

SITCHIN'S COSMOLOGY AND 'PLANET X'

Having said all that, my more recent research suggests there's really no enigma here at all. Admittedly two alternative researchers have gone along with Sitchin in assuming it to be Sumerian, insisting that it represents the sky at the time of the Kofels asteroid strike in 3100 BCE.[17] But other, modern, professional scholars seem to have had little trouble in interpreting it as using Akkadian script all along, and representing the night sky over Nineveh on 3–4 January, 650 BCE.[18]

MORE ON 'PLANET NIBIRU'

Let us briefly review the remainder of the points Sitchin makes about Nibiru itself.[19] First, he insists that its retrograde orbit takes it between Jupiter and Mars. This is partly based on its supposed position on cylinder seal VA243 mentioned above. But he also cites unnamed astronomical texts that 'list the planets in their celestial order', although here he's relying on the name Marduk rather than Nibiru. He adds to this extracts from the *Epic of Creation*: one in which Nibiru supposedly 'holds the central position' – that is, supposedly divides the other planets, excluding the Sun, into two groups of five; the other in which it 'in the midst of Tiamat keeps crossing' – that is, returns to the original position of Tiamat. He is definitely referring here to the following passage in Tablet VII as translated by Dalley, which relates to the use of Neberu, not Nibiru, as one of Marduk's fifty epithets:[20]

> NEBERU: he does indeed hold the crossings of heaven and earth.
> Neither up nor down shall they cross over; they must wait on him.
> Neberu is his star which is bright in the sky.
> He *controls the crossroads*; they must look to him,
> Saying: 'He who *kept crossing inside Tiamat* without respite,
> Shall have Neberu as his name, grasping her middle...'

The relevant lines used by Sitchin are in italics, and for once we can see that his translation is nowhere near as distorted as usual. Moreover, while I can find no proper deconstruction of the word Nibiru/Neberu, Dalley does suggest that it means 'crossing place' –

although she identifies it with the planet Jupiter itself.[21]

Second, in answering the question as to why we've not yet observed such a large planet in the inner solar system, Sitchin uses a variety of textual references to suggest that it has a highly elliptical orbit that takes it deep into space at its apogee – that is, its furthest point from the Sun.[22] From the *Epic of Creation* he quotes that Marduk 'established an outstanding abode'; this is so innocuous I've not even traced it to check its accuracy against Dalley's version. From Job 26:10 he quotes: 'Upon the Deep the Lord marked out an orbit; where light and darkness merge is his farthest limit', whereas the Authorised King James Version says 'He hath compassed the waters with bounds, until the day and night come to an end'; not much similarity there, so perhaps this is yet another of his creative translations, this time of the original Hebrew. Finally from Psalms he quotes: 'From the end of heavens The Lord emanates, and his circuit is to their end'; I couldn't even trace this passage, but it's hardly conclusive even if the rendering is anywhere near accurate. Altogether then, not exactly a strong set of supporting evidence.

Third, one of the chief units of Mesopotamian time measurement was the 3600-year 'sar', and Sitchin suggests that this measure derives from the periodic return of Nibiru from its deep-space orbit.[23] His argument is that its appearance held so much significance for the Ancients that, having recorded its orbital period over many millennia and measured it at 3600 years, they designated the sar to represent this number. He further cites the apparent fact that it was written as a large circle, and that 'the epithet for the planet – *shar* or "supreme ruler" – also meant a "perfect circle" or "completed cycle"'. Of course this could represent a piece of brilliant intuition, but somehow I doubt it.

It would be a mercy to leave this analysis of Sitchin's cosmology here and return to something more constructive. However, because Sitchin himself makes such a song and dance about it, and because his supporters have well and truly jumped on the bandwagon, we must turn our attention to some findings made after *The Twelfth Planet* was published, which appear at first sight to support his claims of Nibiru's existence. A number of modern astronomers have suggested that an additional *tenth* planet – counting properly and ignoring the Sun and Moon – might indeed be lurking far out in our solar system...

THE SEARCH FOR 'PLANET X'

Right back in 1894 the American astronomer Percival Lowell noticed slight irregularities in the orbits of Uranus and Neptune, and proposed that they must derive from the gravitational pull of a more distant object he dubbed 'Planet X' – which reflected both the number ten and its unknown status.[24] This was followed by a considerable lull until, in the late 1970s, after recent revelations about Pluto, the search began in earnest. This was spearheaded by two astronomers at the US Naval Observatory in Washington, Robert Harrington and Tom Van Flandern. They commenced with computer simulations, but observation was also attempted when NASA linked up with them in 1982 and announced that one of the objectives of the Infrared Astronomical Satellite (IRAS) would be to scan the skies for Planet X.

In *Genesis Revisited* Sitchin attached great weight to subsequent announcements made in the press – and two in particular. The first was reported in the *Washington Post* of 30 December 1983.[25] Note that the italics in this and subsequent quotes are mine, for emphasis:

> A heavenly body possibly as large as the giant planet Jupiter and possibly so close to Earth that it would be part of this solar system has been found in the direction of the constellation of Orion... [by IRAS]... *astronomers do not know if it is a planet, a giant comet, a protostar... or a distant galaxy...* 'All I can tell you is that we don't know what it is,' said Gerry Neugebauer, chief IRAS scientist... Conceivably it could be the tenth planet that astronomers have searched for in vain.

A proper reading of this announcement reveals it was hardly conclusive proof that Planet X had been found. However Sitchin put what he termed the 'official denials' down to a government conspiracy to withhold information that was in fact shaping the end of the cold war, as the two superpowers combined to ward of the threat of imminent extraterrestrial invasion. He also inferred that his own theories were ignored by the establishment as part of a cover-up, and used an assortment of contrived arguments to insist that, although the multitude of satellites and probes launched in recent years and planned for the future had been officially searching for planets in neighbouring solar systems, in reality they were concentrating closer to home. However many teams of astronomers were involved in reviewing the IRAS data, and wrote about it at great length – which certainly didn't give it the feel of a cover-up.

The second announcement was reported in *Newsweek* of 13 July 1987:[26]

> NASA held a press conference last week to make a rather strange announcement: an eccentric 10th planet may – *or may not* – be orbiting the Sun. John Anderson, a NASA research scientist who was the principal speaker, has a *hunch* Planet X is out there, though *nowhere near the other nine*.

So, not only was this putative planet not in the right place, but also *hunch* was absolutely the right word. Mark Littmann, a former director of the Hansen Planetarium in Salt Lake City, provided a more detailed explanation in *Planets Beyond: Discovering the Outer Solar System*, published in 1988. He reported that what Anderson had done was observe the *lack* of gravitational effects on the Pioneer 10 and 11 craft – which were by then well into the outer reaches of our solar system – and from this *negative* evidence postulated the *possibility* of a tenth planet that *would have had to have* a highly elliptical and inclined orbit to produce no effect.[27] Given that he'd only recently become converted to the idea of a tenth planet by the purely *theoretical* 'irregular orbit' argument – having previously been a sceptic – this is about as unconvincing as 'evidence' gets.

Returning to Harrington and Van Flandern, both were courted assiduously by Sitchin and his supporters because of the scientific support their work supposedly gave to his theories – and he quoted from their work as if the existence of Planet X was almost a foregone conclusion. In addition to the press reports above, he detailed numerous predictions about Planet X. This culminated in him suggesting that Harrington's team believed that 'the tenth planet is about five times larger than Earth and about three times farther from the Sun than Neptune or Pluto', and that they'd initiated all manner of searches of the skies, providing detailed instructions on where to look. Yet when we consult Van Flandern's own book, *Dark Matter, Missing Planets and New Comets*, published three years after *Genesis Revisited* in 1993, perhaps unsurprisingly we obtain a rather different picture:[28]

> Certainly if such a 'Planet X' *were to be discovered* in a highly inclined and eccentric orbit that approached Neptune's orbit at perihelion and has a mass near the interesting range of 2–5 Earth masses, its existence would argue strongly for the essential correctness of the whole scenario just described [regarding the development of Neptune's satellite system]. A planet in the 2–5 Earth mass range... *could* explain the observed irregularities in the planet orbits if it were presently located 50 to 100 times further from the Sun than the Earth's orbit.

This is as explicit as Van Flandern got in his book, and hardly suggested the definitive distance, size, and orbital path and plane that Sitchin would've had us believe. What is more, as far as the orbital period was concerned, all the studies seemed to work on the basis of something like 500–1000 years, substantially lower than Sitchin's 3600. To top this off Van Flandern indicated that further study of the orbits of a number of comets beyond Neptune – and possibly detailed changes to the laws of gravity – would be required before the mathematical calculations could properly predict the location in which observational searches for Planet X should concentrate – 'if it exists'.[29] Primarily because of this dissatisfaction with the theoretical data at that point, he didn't mention the IRAS observational programme at all. By contrast Harrington remained somewhat sceptical about the orbital irregularity data, and was therefore more inclined to use the 'brute force' mass computation and observational method – although with, in his own words, 'nothing to show for my efforts'.[30]

A number of other groups were engaged in the search for Planet X around this time, all of which pursued different logic and came up with different conclusions. These studies were thoroughly catalogued by Littmann.[31] In particular he quoted a number of experts who felt that reliance on the apparent deviations in the orbits of Uranus and Neptune to predict the existence of a tenth planet was misguided. He himself argued that the deviations were extremely small, and that their analysis relied on data gathered over several centuries – the implication being that the older data, collected using many different systems that had to be converted to a common reference frame, might well have suffered from inaccuracies. E Myles Standish Jr, of the Jet Propulsion Laboratory in California, even reported that these older observations suggested irregularities in the orbits of *all* the planets, which led him to ask: 'Did Planet X visit each one on a grand tour'?[32] However, in fairness we should remind ourselves that Van Flandern based his views not only on the orbital irregularities of Neptune, but also of a number of comets beyond it.

But arguably the real nail in the coffin for Planet X came in 1992, the year before Van Flandern published his work and only a few months before Harrington passed on. Standish showed that the supposed discrepancies in Uranus' orbit had been the result of overestimating the *mass* of Neptune, and that when this was corrected there was no longer a need to postulate a Planet X.[33] It seems this was pretty much accepted by all astronomers at the time.

To bring us right up to date with research conducted since I originally wrote the paper on which this chapter is based, although things went relatively quiet after Standish's revelation, in 2016 Konstantin Batygin and Michael Brown of the California Institute of Technology returned to the theme of a giant planet tracing an unusual, elongated orbit in the outer reaches of our solar system.[34]

SITCHIN'S COSMOLOGY AND 'PLANET X'

This was again, however, only a *theoretical* deduction, this time based on computer modelling of the orbits of smaller objects in the distant Kuiper Belt. The calculations suggested it might have a mass about 10 times that of Earth, with an orbit on average about 20 times further from the Sun than that of Neptune. Not only was there again no suggestion that its potential orbit would take it *between* any of our existing planets, but the distance proposed was absolutely huge – producing an orbital period of somewhere between 10–20,000 years.

I propose we can draw only one valid conclusion from all this. Planet X may indeed exist, as for that matter may Planet XI and others. But it hasn't yet been definitively discovered and observed. Furthermore the huge variety of theoretical postulations concerning its properties don't lend great credence to Sitchin's claims that its orbital eccentricity, plane and period are so well defined that they confirm the details of what the Sumerians were supposedly recording many millennia ago.

Perhaps more important that all of this, though, there remains an essential aspect of this debate that we've so far ignored: *it's only if an additional planet could support life that its existence or otherwise would be of any real relevance to Sitchin's theme...*

LIFE ON PLANET X?

In considering this question, let's first see what Sitchin himself has to say:[35]

> The notion that the only source of energy and heat available to living organisms is the Sun's emissions has been discarded. Thus, the spacecraft Pioneer 10 discovered that Jupiter, though much farther away from the Sun than Earth, was so hot that it must have its own sources of energy and heat. A planet with an abundance of radioactive elements in its depths would not only generate its own heat; it would also experience substantial volcanic activity. Such volcanic activity provides an atmosphere. If the planet is large enough to exert a strong gravitational pull, it will keep its atmosphere almost indefinitely. Such an atmosphere, in turn,

creates a hothouse effect: it shields the planet from the cold of outer space, and keeps the planet's own heat from dissipating into space.

What are we to make of this? Sitchin is quite right to propose that Jupiter has its own internal heat source, a remnant of the way in which it was formed, and the same is true of Saturn. But they are referred to as 'gas giants' for a reason. *They have no solid surface*, simply a small core comprised of molten rock. Not only that but temperatures vary enormously – for example, on Jupiter they range from −145°C in the upper atmosphere to 35,500°C at the core.[36] This produces ferocious and widespread storms, with winds in excess of 370 mph that can rage for centuries and span as much as 1250 miles in diameter. The atmospheric pressure is also orders of magnitude greater than that on Earth. By contrast the two big 'ice giants', Uranus and Neptune, have no internal heat, and underneath their atmospheres are primarily composed of liquid gasses and slushy ice all the way through to their rocky central cores. Most important they too have no solid surface. Moreover all four of these planets have atmospheres very different from Earth, consisting mainly of hydrogen and helium.

In fact, according to Littmann both Harrington and Van Flandern themselves understood that Planet X couldn't possibly support human-like life:[37] 'He [Harrington] and Van Flandern still agree that Planet X should be a frozen methane, ammonia, and water world somewhat like Uranus and Neptune.'

Nor were these the only objections. As Hafernik pointed out, if Planet X had the degree of elliptical orbit that Sitchin and others suggested, then especially at its apogee it would be orders of magnitude further from the Sun than at its perigee.[38] So not only would it be in complete darkness for much if not all of the time, but temperature fluctuations would be even more pronounced. This was born out by the following report that appeared in the *Sunday Times* of 27 October 1996:

> A new planet with an egg-shaped orbit has been discovered by American astronomers. It orbits Cygni B, a star resembling our own

Sun. William Cochrane, the head of the team that discovered the new planet, is baffled. 'We do not understand how it could have formed like this,' he says. *'The new planet has a wildly changeable temperature as it swoops close to the star, then moves out into the far reaches of its solar system.'* This elliptical orbit is similar to that postulated for Planet X by astronomers such as Tom Van Flandern. Its [the new planet's] 'discovery' is mathematical rather than visible, which places it in exactly the same category as Planet X.

Massive fluctuations in temperature, violent storms, an atmosphere made up of totally different gasses, little if any light from the Sun – and, above all, no solid surface. If the Anunnaki were a race of beings who genetically created us 'in their own image', does this sound like their ideal home? Once again a vital piece of Sitchin's jigsaw appears to be a very poor fit.

THE 'NIBIRU CATACLYSM'

The other major change since I originally wrote the paper on which this chapter is based has been the use of Sitchin' original work in an even more outlandish way. Enter the fray Nancy Lieder, a Californian with a full-time job and family who, in 1993, apparently became aware that she was a contactee of a race of 'grey' aliens called Zetans.[39] By 1995 she had set up her own website containing their communications.[40] These opened with a claim that comet Hale-Bopp was in fact a distant star – which wasn't a very good start considering it did indeed turn out to be an extremely bright comet. But that wasn't all. Hale-Bopp was supposedly part of a fraud perpetuated by those in power to distract from the imminent arrival of Planet X, said to be four times the size of Earth, which would pass close enough to us to cause a physical pole shift and crustal displacement – resulting in massive loss of life. The initial date given for this event was apparently 27 May 2003. What is more the whole thing came to be associated with Sitchin's Nibiru – not by Lieder herself, but by conspiracy theorists who picked up on her messages. They seemed oblivious to the fact that Sitchin had never suggested any sort of near-collision with the planet in the future.

Talk of pole shifts and crustal displacement wasn't new – it had previously been proposed in relation the end of the last Ice Age.[41] Nor was the phenomenon of dire warnings of imminent catastrophe, contained in channelled and similar communications, missing their deadlines. May 2003 came and went, with no Planet X. Perhaps sensibly Lieder herself never specified a new date for the cataclysm, although her website is still very much up and running. But others then filled the gap by associating her event with the widespread predictions of catastrophe that were scheduled to accompany the end of the long count of the Mayan Calendar on 21 December 2012.

This date, too, was of course missed. But that didn't deter a 'Christian numerologist' from America who goes by the name of David Meade, although apparently that's only a pseudonym. He revived the topic by tying the Nibiru cataclysm into secret numerological codes contained in the Bible and in the dimensions of the Great Pyramid – things of which, sadly, I have all too much experience from my research into Volume 1 of this series, *Giza: The Truth*. He managed to gain significant media attention for his claims, not least by using the relatively modern phenomenon of social media to spread fake news stories in which NASA supposedly confirmed that Nibiru was heading straight for the Earth. Meade's revised date was the autumn of 2017. Needless to say...

CONCLUSION

Sitchin's theory of the creation of Earth, and of the role Nibiru supposedly played in it, is undeniably incorrect – both from a theoretical standpoint, and because it's far too literal an interpretation of the *Epic of Creation*. Nor do his linguistic and other arguments that the Anunnaki were a race of extraterrestrials from Nibiru hold much water.

Meanwhile an additional 'Planet X' *may* yet be discovered by modern astronomers searching for it based on *theoretical* evidence. But it *hasn't* been discovered yet, and theories about its orbital properties vary widely – so even if one day it is found, it's highly unlikely that it will support Sitchin's detailed theories. More than any of this, though, it's virtually impossible that human-like life could have evolved and prospered on any such planet inhabiting the very outer reaches of our solar system – meaning it couldn't possibly be the 'home of the gods'.

10

SITCHIN'S PANTHEON OF GODS

In chapter 2 we looked at the two main groups in the Sumerian pantheon, the Anunnaki and the Igigi, and at the confusing and often conflicting hierarchical structures relating the two used in different texts. In *The Twelfth Planet* Sitchin rarely refers to the latter, normally using Anunnaki as a blanket term covering all the gods – so, although he does occasionally distinguish them from the 'twelve great gods', this is already something of an over-simplification. In *Genesis Revisited* he makes a half-hearted attempt to rectify this error by acknowledging the separate roles of the two ascribed in the *Epic of Creation*, but then states categorically that 600 Anunnaki were installed on Earth while 300 Igigi remained in orbit in heaven.[1] Not only is this a misreading of the relevant section of Tablet VI of the text – which states there were 600 *in total*, i.e., 300 of each – but also he completely ignores the conflicting statements in separate parts of this and other texts.

However there is an underlying rationale to Sitchin's assembly of the Sumerian pantheon. He suggests the existence of a 'cryptographic numbering system' by which mechanism the 'pantheon of twelve great gods' can be established. He suggests that the names of gods are substituted in certain texts by numbers that identify their numerical rank, using the quasi-sexagesimal system.[2] He further suggests that the pantheon had to remain at twelve, so that only when a member died could one of their offspring step into their shoes, thereby also taking over their numerical rank. Although this sounds perfectly plausible I've found no mention of such a ranking system in the work of the orthodox scholars at all, and of course Sitchin provides no reference as to the source of his theory. There is a passage in the *Gudea Temple Inscriptions* in which Ninurta/Ningirsu is referred to as having been 'invested with fifty offices' by his father Enlil – which, given the latter's supposed ranking of 50 in Sitchin's system, would appear to support the idea of it being passed on.[3] However in the later *Epic of Creation* Marduk is similarly given fifty titles that in this case are recorded in full, and since his supposed father Enki's rank is only 40 this doesn't appear to match Sitchin's system.[4]

We also looked at my reconstruction of the Sumerian pantheon's 'family tree' in chapter 2, and noted that it must be regarded as an approximation rather than a literal set of relationships. The only other attempt at this I've come across was made by Sitchin himself, but as we'll see he seems to make a great many assumptions and oversimplifications, and is often extremely inconsistent from one book to the next.[5]

Among a great many other examples, perhaps the best case study of this is his treatment of Enki's supposed sons. In *The Twelfth Planet* he lists three, Marduk, Dumuzi and Nergal. Now, we know that the first of these is a very late addition to the pantheon who is only recorded as Enki's son in the Akkadian *Epic of Creation*, while I can find little evidence to suggest that the second and third are Enki's sons at all. Then by the time of *The Wars of Gods and Men* he's referring to *six* sons of Enki, although he proceeds to only list five: Marduk, Dumuzi, Nergal, Gibil and the little-known Ninagal.[6] Then again when we come to *The Lost Realms* we find him introducing perhaps the missing sixth son, Ningishzida, to whom he ascribes a great deal of significance by assimilating him with the Egyptian god of wisdom and knowledge, Thoth, the Greek Hermes.[7] Yet Ningishzida isn't one of the celebrated Mesopotamian deities – in chapters 4 and 5 we only came across him once, as one of the gatekeepers of heaven in *Adapa* – which wouldn't appear to justify such a lofty assimilation. For what it's worth he also assimilates the latecomer Marduk with the equally pivotal Egyptian deity Ra.

To put all this into context, Sitchin suggests that An was a remote figure who visited the Earth only occasionally – with the return of Nibiru every 3600 years – to the accompaniment of great pomp and circumstance, leaving Enlil in charge on a day-to-day basis. He further suggests that originally An's first-born son Enki colonised the Earth, but that his command was subsequently usurped by Enlil – the latter being superior by virtue of having been sired by An's half-sister, and thus of purer genetic stock. According to Sitchin this led to great animosity between the two brothers, spawning the rivalry between the 'Enki-ite' and 'Enlil-ite' clans that he claims, as we saw in chapter 7, continued through successive generations and shaped many of the events of the Earth's formative years.

So we can now see that his detailed reconstructions are heavily dependent on knowing to which clan any particular deity belonged. Yet his 'allocations' to these clans are littered with assumptions and inconsistencies. The result? His entire edifice comes tumbling down.

11

CONCLUSION

I have already explained that the reason I've devoted a not insubstantial amount of time and effort to refuting the theories of Zecharia Sitchin is because I believe that, over a number of years, they've misled a great many people about matters of great significance. What is more this clearly isn't just a historic phenomenon. His influence is still strongly felt today in 'Ancient Astronaut' circles and, although he and Erich von Däniken were – and continue to be – by far its most influential proponents, a number of other authors have followed his lead: for example, Alan Alford, Michael Tellinger and Jan Erik Sigdell.[1] To the extent that I was introduced to the fascination of Ancient Mesopotamia by his work, I do owe him some debt of gratitude. What is more, had his vivid reconstructions been presented in novel form, we could perhaps enjoy them as harmless entertainment. But they're not.

No one likes to be misled. It is bad enough if the perpetrator is just mistaken. But if they know exactly what they're doing and undertake their task consciously and willingly, it's a whole lot worse. I concede there's a minute possibility that somehow Sitchin so managed to convince himself he was on the right track that he consciously blinded himself to all the selective evidence building and contorted arguments that ensued. I have potentially seen this happen before. But, as I say, I believe this to only be the minutest of possibilities.

So what's the big deal if people are taken on a wild goose chase about our origins and our ancient past, I hear some say? Why not take it as a bit of harmless fun? I have two answers to this. First, surely the search for truth is important? Especially in an age where it's becoming harder and harder to find, and where most people seem to adopt the stance that any old view is just as valid as any other. If we had always taken this lazy attitude our scientific and other progress would have been significantly slower. As I pointed out in chapter 7, in most areas of research such things as scholarship and peer review do take us much closer to 'truth' than people just chucking ideas around with no real understanding or knowledge. What is more this approach can and should be adopted in alternative and quasi- alternative as much as in orthodox areas of research.

My second and perhaps even more important answer, though, is this. Sitchin's major claim is that we were created by the Anunnaki and that they can and will return – in essence, therefore, that we're a slave race under their total control. As I said in the Preface, this dangerous proposition perpetuates the view that humanity must look outside of itself for its eventual salvation or destruction – whereas I strongly believe that, just as for each of us individually, our collective fate lies entirely in our own hands via faith in our own divinity.

So what is my own view of the Ancient Mesopotamians? Well, there's no doubt that they achieved a level of sophistication that clearly presages our modern civilisation. As for their texts, as I indicated in chapter 3, I take the view that there are certain passages that deserve close scrutiny: from an esoteric standpoint I'd be inclined to single out the multiple references to the 'creation of humankind', and from a more prosaic perspective the multiple versions of the Flood story. These are mirrored in the sacred literature of other ancient civilisations and cultures from all around the world and – lest I be accused of refuting the theories of others without substituting something positive in return – the result of my research into these global texts and traditions can be found in Volume 2 of this series, *Atlantis: The Truth*.[2]

SOURCE REFERENCES

Publication details for the books referenced below can be found in the bibliography. All website references were accurate at the time of original publication. Wherever possible the most up-to-date and readily available English translations of ancient texts, as prepared by orthodox scholars, have been used. Biblical references are taken from the Authorized King James Bible unless otherwise stated.

PREFACE
1. Lawton and Ogilvie-Herald, *Giza: The Truth*, chapter 2, pp. 88–101.

PART ONE: ANCIENT MESOPOTAMIA

1 INTRODUCTION
1. For example see Lawton, *Atlantis: The Truth*, chapter 9, pp. 137–9.
2. Although, for example, Feuerestein et al. argue that the Indus civilisation is earlier in *In Search of the Cradle of Civilisation*.
3. Kramer, *The Sumerians*, chapter 2, pp. 39–40.
4. The information that follows comes primarily from ibid., chapter 3.
5. Ibid., chapter 8, p. 276. Kramer argues that Magan and Meluhha, which are frequently mentioned in texts from earliest times as places with whom Sumer had important trade connections, correspond to Egypt and Ethiopia. Previously scholars had attempted to get round the problem that this implied an advanced seafaring capability by claiming that, originally, these names referred to lands on the much nearer east and south-east Arabian coasts, and that their usage was subsequently translocated. Kramer finds this unlikely, as do I. It is interesting to note that Sumerologist Thorkild Jacobsen goes as far as to say that 'modern scholars tend to think that in earlier times Meluhha denoted India', which would make the seafaring capability all the more impressive (*The Harps that Once...*, p. 363, note 7).
6. Ibid., Appendix I, pp. 340–2.
7. Of the form 'name of owner's patron god, or ruler; owner's name; owner's father's name; owner's title'.
8. As expressed in Kramer, *The Sumerians*, chapter 7.
9. See Map 2 in Roux, *Ancient Iraq*.

10. Kramer, *The Sumerians*, chapter 2.
11. Roux, *Ancient Iraq*, 'Chronological Tables'.

2 THE PANTHEON OF GODS
1. Smith, *The Chaldean Account of Genesis*, chapter 4.
2. Kramer, *The Sumerians*, chapter 4, pp. 122–3.
3. An invaluable source in this exercise was Dalley, *Myths from Mesopotamia*, Glossary, pp. 317–331.
4. Uniquely the name Dumuzi appears a second time in the list, under the sobriquet 'the fisherman', this time for the 4th ruler of the 1st Dynasty of Uruk, but this is less likely to be the figure who was deified.
5. Ezekiel 8:14.

3 THE LITERARY TEXTS
1. For example see Dalley, *Myths from Mesopotamia*, p. 177, note 11.
2. In *The Sumerians*, Appendix B, Kramer describes the Sumerian language as 'agglutinative', in that parts of words retain their individual meaning, so monosyllabic words are often combined to form polysyllabic ones – this is usually denoted in our script by a hyphen between the syllables. By contrast in 'inflected' languages – for example, Indo-European and Semitic ones – roots and vowels change, for example to reflect different tenses, as in *sing, sang, sung*.
3. In ibid., Appendix A, Kramer describes how the development of writing in Mesopotamia went through 5 stages: 1) In the earliest 'pictographic' script dating to *c.* 3000 BCE, each symbol corresponded to a pictorial representation of the object concerned; this required a large number of complicated symbols, although they were gradually simplified in style and reduced in number by substituting phonetic for ideographic values, i.e. if one word sounded like another word, the same symbol was used. 2) The second stage involved laying the symbols on their sides, i.e. rotating them through 90 degrees, purely to facilitate the layout of the writing. 3) The third stage is referred to as 'Archaic' script and dates to *c.* 2500 BCE. This had begun to look like cuneiform proper in as much as the pictures had become stylised and wedge shapes were used throughout. 4) The fourth stage emerged *c.* 1800 BCE, at which point the symbols were further simplified. 5) Ditto the fifth stage *c.* 1000 BCE.
4. Jacobsen, *The Harps that Once…*, Introduction, p. xv.

SOURCE REFERENCES

5. Several of these of varying quality and detail are accessible on the internet. A valuable page with links to Sumerian and Akkadian lexicons and a variety of other useful Mesopotamian sites can be found at www.sumerian.org/sumlinks.htm.
6. The *Akkadisches Handworterbuch* prepared by W Von Soden, and the *Chicago Assyrian Dictionary*.
7. More specifically in chapters 7 and 8.

4 THE SUMERIAN TEXTS

1. Kramer, *The Sumerians*, chapter 5.
2. Jacobsen, *The Harps that Once...*, pp. 145–150.
3. Ibid., pp. 151–166.
4. Ibid., pp. 181–204.
5. Kramer, *The Sumerians*, chapter 4, pp. 148–9.
6. Ibid., chapter 4, pp. 160–162.
7. Ibid., chapter 4, p. 116.
8. Ibid., chapter 5, pp. 171–183.
9. Jacobsen, *The Harps that Once...*, pp. 205–232.
10. Ibid., pp. 3–84.
11. Ibid., pp. 167–180.
12. Ibid., pp. 233–272.
13. Kramer, *The Sumerians*, chapter 5, p. 171.
14. Note that according to the *King List*, Dumuzi reigned as part of this dynasty between Lugalbanda and Gilgamesh. However because he was so extensively deified the works in which he appears are classed as myths.
15. Jacobsen, *The Harps that Once...*, pp. 275–319.
16. Kramer, *The Sumerians*, chapter 8, p. 275.
17. Ibid., chapter 8, pp. 272–3.
18. Jacobsen, *The Harps that Once...*, pp. 320–344.
19. Kramer, *The Sumerians*, chapter 5, p. 185.
20. Ibid., chapter 5, pp. 190–7.
21. Ibid., chapter 5, pp. 197–205.
22. Ibid., chapter 5, pp. 186–190 and Jacobsen, *The Harps that Once...*, pp. 345–355.

23. Jacobsen, *The Harps that Once...*, pp. 101–111.
24. Ibid., pp. 112–124.
25. Kramer, *The Sumerians*, chapter 5, pp. 205–6.
26. Smith, *The Chaldean Account of Genesis*, chapter 10, pp. 160–2; see also Genesis 11:2–7.
27. Jacobsen, *The Harps that Once...*, pp. 288–9, note 25.
28. Ibid., p. 290.
29. Ibid., pp. 386–444.
30. Ibid., pp. 359–374.
31. Ibid., pp. 88–98.

5 THE AKKADIAN TEXTS

1. Because all of these texts are taken from Dalley's work and are easy to locate therein, I don't provide specific references for each.
2. We saw in the last chapter that Kramer suggests these objects were a drum and drumstick. Dalley adds that they were also used in some form of game similar to hockey, which possibly had some link to fertility (*Myths from Mesopotamia*, p. 126, note 8). Whatever the explanation, their significance in this tale remains somewhat enigmatic. It should also be noted that the older Sumerian version has a first part that's omitted from this tablet, so the loss of these objects to the netherworld doesn't follow directly on from Gilgamesh's losing the 'tree of life', as might at first appear.
3. This is again something I discuss in more detail in the relevant companion volume. More generally, though, Berossus is an important figure for anyone attempting to make sense of Mesopotamian literature. He was a Babylonian historian and priest of Bel Marduk who copied out many Akkadian and other texts in Greek in his *Babyloniaca*, written c. 281 BCE. Unfortunately only fragments of this original work survive, but it's quoted by a number of later writers in the 2nd and 1st centuries BCE including Abydenus, Alexander Polyhistor and Appolodorus. Of course we face the usual problems of editing and interpretation of his original by these subsequent authors, and indeed by Berossus himself of the originals. The key issue is that he had access to texts that were subsequently lost and that we've not yet recovered, so his work can on occasions fill important gaps and shed new light.
4. It is interesting to note that Heidel's translation appears to have an

SOURCE REFERENCES

extra 20 lines at the end, wherein Adapa is referred to as the 'seed of humankind' (*The Babylonian Genesis*, Appendix, pp. 152–3). Heidel is at pains to point out that this shouldn't be taken to mean he was the first ever man, similar to the biblical Adam, as some have suggested – because there are abundant references in the story to previous humans.

5. II Kings 2:11.

PART 2: ZECHARIA SITCHIN

6 INTRODUCTION

1. Extract from an interview conducted in 1993 by *Connecting Link*, and published in Issue 17.

7 SITCHIN''S SUPPOSED SCHOLARSHIP

1. I refuse to name this source because in the course of a brief correspondence he made his views on Sitchin's work abundantly clear, stating that he didn't want his name associated with what he regards as 'rubbish', and nor did he want to be bothered by further correspondence from people he regards as cranks. I fully respect his wishes, and have only provided what scant information I have so that I can't be accused of making this important evidence up. The newsgroup postings themselves are long gone.
2. Sitchin, *The Twelfth Planet*, chapter 4, p. 105.
3. See his superb website www.sitchiniswrong.com.
4. Sitchin, *The Twelfth Planet*, chapter 2, p. 42; the reference is to Figure 15 therein.

8 WHAT'S IN A SHEM?

1. Sitchin, *The Twelfth Planet*, chapter 5, p. 136.
2. Ibid., chapter 5, p. 136.
3. Jacobsen, *The Harps that Once…*, Introduction, p. xiv.
4. Kramer, *The Sumerians*, chapter 5, p. 192 and Sitchin, *The Twelfth Planet*, chapter 5, pp. 146–7.
5. Sitchin, *The Twelfth Planet*, chapter 5, p. 134.
6. Ibid., chapter 5, p. 136.
7. Jacobsen, *The Harps that Once…*, p. 444.

8. Sitchin, *The Twelfth Planet*, chapter 5, pp. 144–5.
9. Heidel, *The Babylonian Genesis*, Appendix, p. 151.
10. Dalley, *Myths from Mesopotamia*, p. 187.
11. Dalley, *Myths from Mesopotamia*, p. 196 and Sitchin, *The Twelfth Planet*, chapter 5, p. 151.
12. Dalley, *Myths from Mesopotamia*, p. 207 and Sitchin, *The Twelfth Planet*, chapter 4, p. 104.
13. I quote from his personal correspondence dated 15 Dec 2001:

    The line (83) that describes Anzu's flight is, in Akkadian:

    an-zu-u ip-pa-ri$-ma KUR-us-su ig-gu$ (where the $ = the 'sh' sound, usually marked with an 's' with a circumflex over it).

    The KUR sign, which is a Sumerogram and isn't an Akkadian word, represents either the Akkadian mat-, 'land' or $ad-, 'mountain'. In this case, the word for mountain is better, so it's best to read: 'Anzu flew and went off to his mountain.'

    Nowhere is the means of Anzu's flight mentioned, nor do we find reference to a 'name' or, in Sumerian, a MU. It is possible that Sitchin, in looking at a copy of the tablet, mistook the KUR for a MU, since the two are similar (they're similarly shaped, though confusing them is not common). However, reading MU-us-su just doesn't make any sense in the context. Literally, the text is 'Anzu flew and (ippari$ma) went towards (iggu$) his KUR/MU'. In either case, the KUR/MU isn't the means of the flying, as Sitchin translates. Instead, it's *where* he is going, as noted by the -us-, which is actually -um-, the locative indicator, plus -$u-, the possessive (i.e. 'his'), which, when put together, assimilate into -ussu-, or 'to his X'. And to say that he 'went to his rocket ship and flew' (thus twisting the word order) is impossible, since the verb napri$u (Akkadian verb 'to fly') is followed by the conjunction -ma, 'and', thus the flying is clearly the first action; the 'going towards' (in Akkadian naga$) is second. And of course, one doesn't fly and then go to the ship: one goes to the ship and then flies, a translation that, given the grammar, just isn't possible.

14. Dalley, *Myths from Mesopotamia*, p. 262.
15. Sitchin, *The Twelfth Planet*, chapter 5, p. 141.
16. Ibid., chapter 5, pp. 159–160.
17. Ibid., chapter 5, pp. 139–140.

18. Ibid., chapter 5, p. 138.
19. Ibid., chapter 5, p. 136.
20. Sitchin, *The Wars of Gods and Men*, chapter 7, pp. 143–5.

9 SITCHIN'S COSMOLOGY AND 'PLANET X'
1. Sitchin, *The Twelfth Planet*, chapters 6–7, pp. 184–188.
2. Ibid., chapter 7, p. 189, Figures 99–101.
3. See www.sitchiniswrong.com/VA243/VA243.htm. The real detail is contained in the downloadable 'VA243seal.pdf'.
4. Towards the end of the above-named paper Heiser lists the eleven books specifically about Mesopotamian astronomy that he consulted regarding his 'five planets only' assertion. Of these eight were written from the 1970s on. By contrast the six main texts Sitchin quotes in support of his 'twelve planets' hypothesis (see *The Twelfth Planet*, chapter 6, pp. 184–5) are significantly older. Although four aren't even listed in his bibliography, my own research reveals the earliest of the six was published in 1892, the most recent in 1934.
5. Sitchin, *The Twelfth Planet*, chapter 7, pp. 191–213.
6. See www.geocities.com/Area51/Corridor/8148/hafernik.html. For 3 years Hafernik also worked on the Space Shuttle as a government contractor for NASA.
7. Sitchin, *The Twelfth Planet*, chapter 8, pp. 222–3.
8. Heidel, *The Babylonian Genesis*, p. 115.
9. Sitchin, *The Twelfth Planet*, chapter 7, pp. 208–9.
10. More specifically in chapter 8.
11. Sitchin, *The Twelfth Planet*, chapter 8, pp. 217–9.
12. Ibid., chapter 8, pp. 218–221.
13. See, for example, http://en.wikipedia.org/wiki/Nephilim (under Etymology).
14. See Sitchin, *The Twelfth Planet*, chapter 5, p. 160 and *Genesis Revisited*, chapter 1, p. 19.
15. Heise is a senior scientist in the High Energy Astrophysics Division of the Space Research Organization Netherlands, but he also provides an Akkadian language dictionary at http://space.tin.it/clubnet/bxpoma/akkadeng/akkadengindex.htm. For Jacobsen's interpretation see *The Harps that Once...*, p. 240, note 10.

16. Sitchin, *Genesis Revisited*, chapter 4, p. 87.
17. See Bond, Alan and Hempsall, Mark, *A Sumerian Observation of the Kofels Impact Event* (WritersPrintShop, 2008).
18. See https://research.britishmuseum.org/research/collection_online/collection_object_details.aspx?objectId=303316.
19. Sitchin, *The Twelfth Planet*, chapter 8, pp. 215–6.
20. Dalley, *Myths from Mesopotamia*, pp. 272–3.
21. Ibid., Glossary, p. 325.
22. Sitchin, *The Twelfth Planet*, chapter 8, pp. 216–7.
23. Ibid., chapter 8, p. 224.
24. See, for example, http://en.wikipedia.org/wiki/Nibiru_catacylsm (under Misappellations then Planet X).
25. Sitchin, *Genesis Revisited*, chapter 13, pp. 319–320; see also the archive for that date at www.washingtonpost.com, under the title 'Possibly as Large as Jupiter'.
26. Ibid., chapter 13, pp. 323–4.
27. Littmann, *Planets Beyond*, chapter 13, p. 204.
28. Van Flandern, *Dark Matter…*, chapter 17, p. 312 and chapter 18, p. 322.
29. Continuing our perusal of Van Flandern's book we find that, although he supported Sitchin's ideas of a 'dynamic' evolution of our solar system, his own theory of its creation was completely at odds with Sitchin's in terms of detail. For example, he supported the commonly-held view that the Moon was formed by splitting off from the Earth, which was itself was one of the original members of our solar system (see ibid., chapter 19, pp. 332–6). Furthermore he argued that there's evidence that a planet separate from Planet X exploded between Mars and Jupiter about 3 million years ago (see ibid., chapter 19, pp. 340–2). But it's perhaps surprising to find that, in a self-acknowledged departure into pure speculation in a book that was otherwise highly rigorous and scientific, he did broadly support the general idea of an extraterrestrial race of gods who, he suggests, came from this latter planet and who, knowing their imminent fate, escaped to Earth, created humankind and passed on their knowledge. This differs from Sitchin's view in that Van Flandern was talking about a totally different planet, one that exploded; the timescales were about 2.5 million years too early; and his gods died out early on, unable to live long-term on Earth due to its different environment.

30. Littmann, *Planets Beyond*, chapter 13, p. 198.
31. Ibid., chapter 13 and Chronological Table, p. 258.
32. Ibid., chapter 13, pp. 216–9.
33. Standish, 'Planet X – No dynamical evidence in the optical observations', *Astronomical Journal* 105:5 (1992), pp. 200–6.
34. Batygin and Brown, 'Evidence for a Distant Giant Planet in the Solar System', *Astronomical Journal* 151:2 (2016).
35. Sitchin, *The Twelfth Planet*, chapter 8, p. 229.
36. See, for example, www.universetoday.com/47968/how-hot-is-jupiter.
37. Littmann, *Planets Beyond*, chapter 13, p. 199.
38. See note 6 above.
39. This comes from her website, www.zetatalk.com/nancybio.htm.
40. Most of the remaining information comes from http://en.wikipedia.org/wiki/Nibiru_catacylsm – because admittedly with only a brief perusal I was unable to find the relevant historical information on Lieder's own website.
41. For example see Lawton, *Atlantis: The Truth*, chapter 12, pp. 201–2.

10 SITCHIN'S PANTHEON OF GODS
1. Sitchin, *Genesis Revisited*, chapter 4, p. 87.
2. Sitchin, *The Twelfth Planet*, chapter 4, p. 119. He suggests the male ranks were as follows: 60 – An, 50 – Enlil, 40 – Enki, 30 – Nanna, 20 – Utu, 10 – Ishkur; and the female ranks were: 55 – Antu, 45 – Ninlil, 35 – Ninki, 25 – Ningal, 15 – Inanna, 5 – Ninhursag.
3. Jacobsen, *The Harps that Once...*, p. 400.
4. In Tablets VI and VII; see Dalley, *Myths from Mesopotamia*, p. 273. Sitchin's counter-argument is that Marduk took over the supreme role of the 'Enlilship', despite supposedly being Enki's son.
5. Sitchin, *The Twelfth Planet*, chapter 4, p. 121.
6. Sitchin, *The Wars of Gods and Men*, chapter 6, pp. 126–7.
7. Sitchin, *The Lost Realms*, chapter 9, p. 183.

11 CONCLUSION
1. See the Bibliography for details of their respective efforts.
2. More specifically in chapters 7 and 8.

BIBLIOGRAPHY

This bibliography is limited to the books specifically referenced in this work. The details given below are for the imprint or edition consulted, although the original date of publication quoted in the main text may have been earlier.

Alford, Alan, *Gods of the New Millennium*, Hodder and Stoughton, 1997.

Dalley, Stephanie, *Myths from Mesopotamia*, Oxford University, 1989.

Feuerestein, Georg, Kak, Subhash and Frawley, David, *In Search of the Cradle of Civilisation*, Quest, 1995.

Heidel, Alexander, *The Babylonian Genesis*, University of Chicago, 1951.

Jacobsen, Thorkild, *The Harps that Once… Sumerian Poetry in Translation*, Yale University Press, 1987.

Kramer, Samuel Noah, *The Sumerians*, University of Chicago, 1963.

Lawton, Ian and Ogilvie-Herald, Chris, *Giza: The Truth*, Rational Spirituality Press, 2020 (first published 1999).

Lawton, Ian, *Atlantis: The Truth*, Rational Spirituality Press, 2020 (originally published as *Genesis* Unveiled in 2003).

Littmann, Mark, *Planets Beyond: Discovering the Outer Solar System*, Wiley and Sons, 1988.

Roux, Georges, *Ancient Iraq*, Penguin, 1992.

Sigdell, Jan Erik, *Reign of the Annunaki*, Bear & Co, 2018.

Sitchin, Zecharia, *The Twelfth Planet*, Bear & Co, 1991 (1st Edition, 1976).

Sitchin, Zecharia, *The Stairway to Heaven*, Avon, 1980.

Sitchin, Zecharia, *The Wars of Gods and Men*, Avon, 1985.

Sitchin, Zecharia, *The Lost Realms*, Avon, 1990.

Sitchin, Zecharia, *Genesis Revisited*, Avon, 1990.

Sitchin, Zecharia, *When Time Began*, Avon, 1993.

Smith, George, *The Chaldean Account of Genesis*, Sampson Low, 1876.

Tellinger, Michael, *Slave Species of the Gods*, Bear & Co, 2012.

Van Flandern, Tom, *Dark Matter, Missing Planets and New Comets*, North Atlantic Books, 1993.

INDEX

Abraham, 16
Abzu or Apsu, 24, 28, 37, 52, 59, 61, 81, 88
Adapa or Oannes, 60–1, 79, 106
Agga or Aka, 22, 47
Akkad, 10, 14–16, 18–20, 22–3, 25–7, 30, 33–7, 47–51, 56, 72, 76–8, 80–1, 86–7, 90, 93–4, 106
An or Anu, 25, 27–8, 36, 50, 53–5, 58, 61, 79, 87–8, 92–3, 107
Alford, Alan, 108
Anderson, John, 97
Anshar, 88
Anunnaki or Igigi, 24–6, 38, 53–4, 61, 65–6, 73, 81, 85, 88, 91–3, 102–3, 105, 109
Anzu or Zu, 24, 27, 52, 62–3, 80–1
Aratta, 44–5, 49
Asalluhe, 27
Ashur, 13, 52–3, 60–1
Ashurbanipal, 13, 23, 30–1, 93
Assyro-Babylonian, 15, 21–4, 26–8, 30–1
Atlantis, 1, 34, 53, 91, 109
Atrahasis, 24, 36–7, 49, 54–5, 61
Azag, 42–3, 62
Babylon, 6, 23, 30–1, 36, 49, 52–4, 56, 61–2, 81, 90–1
Bad-Tibira, 29
Batygin, Konstantin, 99
Bauval, Robert, 69–70
Behistun, 14

Berossus, 60
Bilulu, 43
Birs Nimrud, 49
Botta, Paul Emil, 13
Brown, Michael, 99
Brunow, Rudolph, 16
Dalley, Stephanie, 18, 51, 53–4, 61–2, 79–81, 83, 91, 94–5
Dilmun, 38–9
Dumuzi, 29, 41, 61, 106
Dunnu, 51
Duranki, 48
Egypt, Ancient, 1–2, 5–8, 54, 60, 69
Ekur, 48, 50
Elohim, 31
Enheduanna, 48
Enki, Ea or Nudimmud, 16, 25, 27–8, 36–41, 43, 49–50, 52, 55, 59–61, 73–4, 79, 81, 88, 106–7
Enkidu, 46–7, 56–60, 78
Enlil or Ellil, 16, 20, 25, 27–8, 36, 42–3, 46, 48–50, 52, 54–5, 57–60, 62, 73–4, 80, 106–7
Enmerkar, 22, 44–5, 49
Ereshkigal, 27, 41, 48, 54
Eridu, 16, 22, 39, 43, 73
Etana, 22, 61, 80
Falkenstein, Adam, 18
Gaga, 88
Geb, 90
Genesis, Book of, 5, 25, 36, 48, 56, 67, 73, 90, 96, 98, 105

Gibil, 27, 62, 106
Gilgamesh, 22, 27, 37, 44, 46–7, 56–9, 78
Girsu, 49
Giza, 1–2, 66, 69–70, 83, 103
Gudea, 20, 50, 79, 106
Gutium, 23, 49–50
Hafernik, Rob, 88, 101
Hammurabi, 21, 23
Hancock, Graham, 69–70
Harrington, Robert, 96–9, 101
Heidel, Alexander, 18, 52, 79–80, 90
Heise, John, 92
Heiser, Michael, 73, 86–7
Hendursag, 48
Hermes, 106
Hincks, Edward, 14–15
Huwawa or Humbaba, 46, 57–8
Ibbi-Sin, 21
Inanna or Ishtar, 16, 21, 25, 27–9, 39, 41–5, 47–8, 51, 56, 58, 78–9
Ishbi-Erra, 21, 23
Ishkur or Adad, 27, 62, 73, 83
Ishum, 24, 27, 53, 61
Isin, 21, 23, 28, 36
Isin-Larsa, 23, 28, 36
Jacobsen, Thorkild, 16, 18, 28, 32, 35, 39, 42–3, 45, 47–50, 62, 71, 77–9, 83, 92
K8538, planisphere, 93
Khorsabad, 13
Khufu, 2, 66, 71
King, Leonard, 18
Kingu, 53, 88
Kish, 15, 22, 46–7, 52, 61

Kishar, 88
Kramer, Samuel Noah, 6–7, 12, 18–19, 25, 28, 35, 39–41, 43–8, 83
Kuyunjik, 13
Lagash or Telloh, 15, 20, 49
Lahamu, 88
Lahmu, 88
Lambert, Wilfred, 18, 54
Langdon, Stephen, 15, 18
Larsa, 20
Layard, Austen Henry, 13–14, 31
Lieder, Nancy, 102–3
Littmann, Mark, 97, 99, 101
Lowell, Percival, 96
Lugalbanda, 22, 44–6, 62
Marduk, 27–8, 31, 52–4, 72, 81, 88, 90–1, 94–5, 106
Mesopotamia, 1, 5–6, 11, 13, 15–16, 19–20, 22–3, 31, 38, 41, 51, 56, 81, 87, 91, 108
Millard, Alan, 18, 54
Mummu, 52, 88
Namma, 37
Nanna or Sin, 21, 42–3, 50
Nanna, Sin or Suen, 25, 42–3, 60
Nephilim, 67, 73, 85, 91
Nergal or Erra, 24, 27, 53–4, 61, 106
Nibiru, 66, 73, 88–9, 91, 94–5, 102–3, 107
Nidaba, 48
Nimrud, 13
Ninagal, 106
Nineveh, 13–14, 16, 23, 30–1, 52–4, 56, 61–2, 93–4
Ningishzida, 61, 106

INDEX

Ninhursag, Ninmah or Nintu, 25, 27–8, 36–9, 50, 55–7, 60, 83, 92
Ninisinna, 48
Ninkasi, 11, 48
Ninsikilah or Ninki, 38
Ninsun, 46, 57
Ninurta or Ningirsu, 27, 42–3, 48–9, 62, 79, 106
Nippur, 15, 16, 19–20, 36, 38, 42–3, 46, 48, 50
Nungal, 48
Old Testament, 30–1, 65
Oppert, Julius, 14–15
Persepolis, 14
Planet X, 66, 74, 96–103
Poebel, Arno, 16
Prince, John, 16
Pyramid, the Great, 2, 66, 71, 83, 103
Rassam, Hormuzd, 13
Rawlinson, Henry Creswicke, 14, 25
Roux, Georges, 22
Sargon, 13, 19, 23, 48
Sayce, Archibald, 16
Sennacherib, 23
Shara, 62
Sharur, 42, 62
Shu, 50, 90
Shukalletuda, 43
Shulgi, 31
Shuruppak, 15, 36
Shu-Suen or Shu-Sin, 50
Sigdell, Jan Erik, 108
Sippar, 56
Sitchin, Zecharia, 2-3, 65–109

Smith, George, 13, 18, 25, 48–9
Speiser, Ephraim, 18
Standish, E Myles, 99
Sumer, 6-12, 15–16, 18, 20, 22–8, 30–9, 41, 44, 46–7, 50–4, 56, 58, 60–2, 65–6, 71–4, 76–8, 90, 92–4, 100, 105–6
Tellinger, Michael, 108
Thoth, 106
Thureau-Dangin, Francois, 16
Tiamat, 52, 73, 81, 88–90, 94
Ur, 8, 16, 20–3, 31, 36, 46, 50, 53, 56
Urshanabi, 58
Uruk or Erech, 15–16, 22, 28, 39, 44–7, 54, 57, 59
Utnapishtim, 56, 58–9
Utu or Shamash, 25, 27, 46, 48, 57–8, 61, 80
VA243, cylinder seal, 86, 94
Van Flandern, Tom, 96–9, 101–2
von Däniken, Erich, 69, 108
Vyse, Richard Howard, 2, 71
Woolley, Leonard, 16
Ziusudra, 29, 36

Plate 1: The remains of the Great Ziggurat of Ur, completed by King Shulgi in the 21st century BCE, partially restored in the 6th century BCE, and excavated by Leonard Woolley and others in the early 1900s. More recently Saddam Hussein ordered that the façade and massive staircase be rebuilt. (dreamstime.com)

Plate 2: An Assyrian frieze from King Assurnasirpal's palace at Nimrud. Donated by Henry Layard to the Canford Estate in Dorset in the 1950s, it was plastered over, forgotten and fronted by a dartboard used by prefects at the school in the 1970s and 80s – including myself! It was rediscovered and sold at auction in 1992. (Canford School)

Plate 3: Clay tablet containing part of the celebrated 'Epic of Gilgamesh', written using the distinctive, tight-packed, wedge-shaped, cuneiform script used by the Akkadians. (British Museum)

Plate 4: Clay tablet showing an example of the early Sumerian pictographic script from which later cuneiform developed.

Plate 5: Planisphere K8538, discovered in the ruins of Ashurbanipal's library at Nineveh. (British Museum)

THE PREHISTORIC TRUTH SERIES

all published by Rational Spirituality Press *www.rspress.org*
see also *www.ianlawton.com*

[Volume 1] GIZA: THE TRUTH (2020) is the 20th anniversary edition of this celebrated book, which thoroughly investigates how, why and when the most famous archaeological monuments in the world were built... in the process placing grave doubt on the multitude of alternative theories that surround them.

[Volume 2] ATLANTIS: THE TRUTH (2020) is a reinterpretation of the most revered ancient texts and traditions from all around the world that postulates a forgotten, highly cultured but not technologically advanced 'golden race' who were wiped out in a global catastrophe around 13,000 years ago... with supporting geological and other evidence suggesting where, when and how this 'Atlantean' race most likely lived.

[Volume 3] MESOPOTAMIA: THE TRUTH (2020) is an investigation into what was really going on in what is perhaps the definitive cradle of civilisation, and what elements of modern living were introduced for the first time... coupled with a thorough rebuttal of alternative interpretations of its texts concerning supposed extraterrestrial visitors who genetically created humankind.

THE SUPERSOUL SERIES

all published by Rational Spirituality Press www.rspress.org
see also www.ianlawton.com

RESEARCH BOOKS

[Volume 1] SUPERSOUL (2013) is the main reference book for Supersoul Spirituality, containing out-of-body and channelled evidence that each and every one of us is a holographic reflection of a supersoul that has power way beyond our wildest imaginings.

[Volume 2] THE POWER OF YOU (2014) compares modern channelled wisdom from a variety of well-known sources, all emphasising that each of us is consciously or unconsciously creating every aspect of our own reality, and that this is what the current consciousness shift is all about.

[Volume 3] AFTERLIFE (2019) is a state-of-the-art, clear, reliable guide to the afterlife based on the underlying consistencies in traditional channelled material and modern out-of-body research.

SIMPLE BOOKS

SH*T DOESN'T JUST HAPPEN!! (2016) introduces Supersoul Spirituality by explaining how and why we ourselves create or attract everything we experience in our adult lives... so that we are never victims of chance, God's will, our karma or our life plans.

WHAT JESUS WAS REALLY SAYING (2016) is a fundamental reinterpretation of the Christian message that uses excerpts from the Gospels to propose that, through his supposed miracles, Jesus was trying to show us that each of us is a creator god of the highest order and can manipulate the illusion we call reality at will.

 THE GOD WHO SOMETIMES SCREWED UP (2018) charts the author's progression from motorcycle and car racer, to pyramid explorer and researcher of ancient civilisations, to spiritual philosopher… with analysis and examples of how he has created or manifested all the various aspects of his life, both good and bad.

 DEATH IS AN ADVENTURE!! (2019) is a simple yet essential guide to the afterlife, which answers all your questions such as why you will continue to exist, what to expect and how best to prepare. Based on evidence not belief, it describes the unlimited possibilities we have to create wondrous new experiences… as long as we have a reliable map of the territory.

IAN LAWTON was born in 1959. Formerly an accountant, sales exec, business and IT consultant and avid bike and car racer, in his mid-thirties he changed tack completely to become a writer-researcher specialising in ancient history. His first two books, *Giza: The Truth* and *Genesis Unveiled*, sold over 30,000 copies worldwide.

After this he turned to spiritual philosophy, and in his *Books of the Soul Series* he originated the ideas of Rational Spirituality and of the holographic soul. But since 2013 he has been developing the more radical worldview of Supersoul Spirituality in the *Supersoul Series*. A short film clip discussing the latter can be found at *www.ianlawton.com* and on YouTube.

www.ingramcontent.com/pod-product-compliance
Lightning Source LLC
Chambersburg PA
CBHW070159100426
42743CB00013B/2981